Hebrew with Joy!
in the Biblical Feasts

Hebrew Vocabulary, Scriptures & Traditions of GOD's Appointed Times

Joy Carroll

Hebrew with Joy! in the Biblical Feasts
Hebrew Vocabulary, Scriptures & Traditions of GOD's Appointed Times

©2021 by SimkhaPress
ISBN: 978-1-7333230-4-8

The websites cited in this book were active at time of publishing. There is no guarantee that they
will continue to be available in the future.

For free Video Series, PowerPoints and Audios for use with this book, visit: HebrewWithJoy.com

Hebrew with Joy! in the Biblical Feasts may be purchased at special quantity discounts. For more
information, visit HebrewWithJoy,com or contact Joy at hebrewwithjoy33@gmail.com

Published 12-16-21
Revision 8-17-23

Dedications

Hebrew with Joy! in the Biblical Feasts (HJBF) is dedicated to two amazing women of GOD; Jackie Newman, whose faithful suggestions, prayers, encouragement, and support have been a continual blessing to me and Erin Miskey, who has blessed this book with her incredible wisdom, Hebrew knowledge and attention to editing detail. I could not have written this book without you two! Todah rabah Jackie and Erin!

Todah Rabah (thanks very much) to:
HJBF Prayer Team: Your faithfulness to pray for me through this project provided the encouragement, inspiration, strength and energy to complete HJBF.
Graphic Designer: our wonderful daughter, Becca Kendall
Author Photo: Randie Ide
HJBF Editing, Proofing and Testing Team:
Erin Miskey, Rachel Zoller, Ilene Wallmueller, Scott Koppel,
Jackie Newman's test class: Celeste, Clif, Kat, Krys, Jenny, Michelle, Poony
Joy's test class: Kathy Stephens, Heather Martin, Alleluia Williams,
Julie Bailey, Rhonda Brown, Jackie Newman

Todah rabah (thanks so much) to all of my Hebrew students, who, for many years, have encouraged me to continue teaching and writing and have such a love for the holy language of GOD!

Testimonials

I have had the privilege of experiencing all three *Hebrew with Joy* books, and *Hebrew with Joy! In the Biblical Feasts* does not disappoint! I found *Hebrew with Joy!* one of the **best** introductions to learning the Hebrew language of any Hebrew class I have ever taken! At the end of the book, you will be reading Hebrew if you have applied yourself to the lessons. *Hebrew with Joy! In the Biblical Feasts* is an excellent source in learning new words and Hebrew roots associated with the Feasts of the LORD. The book delineates the Biblical and cultural celebrations of the Feasts and is a most enjoyable learning experience for anyone who holds the Word of אֱלֹהִים dear to their hearts! *Rhonda Brown, Colorado*

Amazon Reviews

5.0 out of 5 stars **An Excellent Teacher**

I went through the lessons. I don't learn things easily because I am a multiple sensory learner. It was easy for me to learn books one and two in Hebrew with Joy. There definitely is studying involved and practicing the lessons. However, Hebrew with Joy makes it as easy as possible for people to learn Hebrew. The books one and two in Hebrew with Joy is a huge reason why I will know how to read the Torah scroll for my Bar Mitzvah. I highly recommend books one and two in Hebrew with Joy. I am extremely looking forward to Book Three.

5.0 out of 5 stars ***Highly recommended!***

After going through the "Hebrew with Joy! Learn Simple Hebrew with the Scriptures" book, I decided to study this one, too, and I am so glad that I did. I made great progress in being able to read Hebrew, and I loved that Joy used the Biblical Feasts as the basis of study. I have taught English as a Foreign Language for several years, and I wish that I had a similar book for teaching English — the vocabulary, roots, review sections, and additional resources that Joy has available are helpful and amazing. I highly recommend this book for learning Hebrew and more about the feasts, and I am looking forward to studying the next book, as well.

5.0 out of 5 stars **An excellent book for increasing your knowledge of Hebrew and the Biblical Feasts**

The author, Joy Carroll, has made this book an extraordinary resource for learning and reading Hebrew by looking at the Biblical Feasts! You will be surprised how quickly you will gain your knowledge of Hebrew and the understanding of the Biblical Feasts as you go through this book!! I highly recommend Hebrew With Joy In the Biblical Feasts!!! You will be blessed by it!!!!

Table of Contents

Introduction

Shalom and welcome to *Hebrew with Joy! in the Biblical Feasts*. This book is designed for Hebrew students who have a desire to learn the vocabulary associated with each Feast and have already learned the Hebrew Alef Bet. If you have not already learned the Hebrew letters and vowels, please complete *Hebrew with Joy!* before moving on to this book.

Free Video Lesson Files are a part of the Hebrew with Joy! learning system. They allow you to study on your own – almost like being right in the classroom! These lessons are helpful for individuals, families, home school, Bible study or other groups. They can be downloaded from this site:

https://hebrewwithjoy.com/hjbf-video-series   PW: HJBFvideos

Free Audio files are so helpful if you are an audio learner. The files can be accessed at https://hebrewwithjoy.com/hjbf-audios/

Flashcards and other Handouts can be downloaded and printed at HebrewWithJoy.com.

Pronunciation *Hebrew with Joy! in the Biblical Feasts* teaches the Sephardic form of pronunciation to honor the standard pronunciation used in Israel.

Suggestions for Students:

- Try to study with a partner or in a group. The accountability and interaction will aid in learning.
- Practice using the flashcards to learn the new vocabulary and grammar (Appendix C).
- Try *not* to write the Hebrew transliterations (English sounds) above the Hebrew in the book! This will slow down the learning process.
- After each lesson is taught, use the learning activity that goes with the lesson. It will reinforce the materials in a fun, up-beat way.
- Listen to the audio files between class sessions to reinforce the new vocabulary as you practice your pronunciation.
- Have fun as you learn the language of GOD!

Suggestions for Teachers:

- Be sure that the students know the Alef-Bet before taking this class. If needed, suggest that they complete the *Hebrew with Joy!* book first.
- Encourage students to use the flashcards to reinforce the new vocabulary and grammar.
- Try to discourage students from writing the Hebrew transliterations (English sounds) above the Hebrew in the book! This will slow down the learning process.
- Allow students to work as partners as much as possible. For example, partners can practice reading and translating with each other before speaking out loud to the class.
- Be sure to call on all students to read out loud.
- When a student is reading out loud and makes a mistake, *first* ask the student to try the word again. Then, if they still struggle, ask if another student can help. As a _last_ resort, the teacher pronounces the word.
- After each lesson is taught, use the learning activity that goes with the lesson. It will reinforce the materials in a fun, up-beat way.
- Encourage students to listen to the audio files between class sessions. This will especially help the auditory learners.
- Video lessons can also be used as a teaching tool. The files are in process and will be available to download in the near future. Check the HebrewWithJoy.com website for updates.

1 – Moving Forward

A – Welcome!

שָׁלוֹם (hello) students! I'm so glad you have joined me for *Hebrew with Joy! in the Biblical Feasts.* This book gives you the opportunity not only to learn about the Feasts, but also to grow your Hebrew knowledge and vocabulary at the same time!

A1

Why study *Hebrew with Joy! in the Biblical Feasts*? There are many books written on the Feasts of the LORD, each with a different purpose and perspective. In this book, our focus is to study the Hebrew words and roots found in the Feasts while exploring the Scriptures, prayers and traditions associated with these קָדוֹשׁ (holy) "mo-a-DEEM" (appointed times) with יְהֹוָה "Adonai" (the LORD).

Growing up in a Jewish home, I experienced many of the Biblical Feasts of the LORD, but I had no understanding about their meaning and beauty. Years later, as I began exploring my Hebraic roots, I began to teach this amazing language of עִבְרִית "eev-REET" (Hebrew), which has led to a deeper understanding and love for Adonai and His appointed times.

"For everything there is a season, a time for every purpose under heaven." Ecclesiastes 3:1

God not only sanctifies <u>people</u> and <u>places</u> but also <u>time</u>. People, places, and time are a three-strand cord held together by the One who sanctifies and makes each holy. King Solomon wrote in his wisdom that God has a divine purpose for each one of His sacred meeting times. Are we missing a blessing by failing to keep our "appointments" with God? Each of these are intended to be celebrations or memorials of Him.

Hannah Nesher   VoiceforIsrael.net

A2

<u>This course assumes you already know the Hebrew letters and vowels. If you haven't taken Hebrew before, please complete *Hebrew with Joy!* before starting this book.</u>

This lesson is a review of the key concepts presented in *Hebrew with Joy!* I have provided a self-quiz on the next page to show you if there are any letters or vowels which you need to review. I have also included the Hebrew Letters and Vowels charts in Appendices A and B.

On the next page, you have an opportunity to review the Hebrew letters and vowels before moving on. I am excited that you have decided to join me in the study of GOD's holy language!

Hebrew Letter and Vowel Self-Quiz

To find out which letters and vowels you need to review, take the following quiz. Write the number of the English sound that matches the Hebrew letter(s). Check the answers below.

A4		
ע ___	1. d	
צ ___	2. r	
פ ___	3. silent	
ר ___	4. s	
ק ___	5. k	
ד ___	6. ts	
ס ___	7. p	

A3		
א __3__	1. m	
ג ___	2. f	
פ ___	3. silent	
שׂ ___	4. l	
כ ___	5. g	
מ ___	6. s	
ל ___	7. kh	

A6		
Numbers can be used more than once!		
תָ___	1. too	
תוֹ___	2. tee	
תַ ___	3. tai (tie)	
תוּ___	4. ta (tah)	
תֵי___	5. to (toe)	
תֶי___	6. te (teh)	
תֶ___	7. tay	
תִי___	8. tooey	
תָ___	9. toy	
תוֹי___		
תוּי___		

A5		
ז ___	1. m	
י ___	2. z	
ה ___	3. b	
שׁ ___	4. sh	
ם ___	5. v	
נ ___	6. h	
ת ___	7. t	
ב ___	8. n	
ח ___	9. y	
ו ___	10. kh (ch)	

A6	from top →	8,9,6,2,6,7,3,1,2,5,4
A5	from top →	5,10,3,7,8,1,4,6,9,2
A4	from top →	4,1,5,2,7,6,3
A3	from top →	4,1,7,6,2,5,3

Are you ready to move forward? Then, join me as we study the קָדוֹשׁ (holy) מוֹעֲדִים (appointed times) of our amazing יְהֹוָה (LORD).

B – Vocabulary

Each lesson includes a list of "עִבְרִית" (Hebrew) words used in that lesson and in upcoming lessons. To help you memorize, cut out the cards in Appendix C or make your own flashcards. You can also download the flashcards from: hebrewwithjoy.com/hjbf-book-handouts/

Memorize each of the following words before moving to the next lesson.

English	Gender*	Transliteration	Hebrew	
GOD, god	*ms/mpl*	e-lo-HEEM	אֱלֹהִים	B1
Hebrew	*fs*	eev-REET	עִבְרִית	B2
holy (adjective)	*ms*	ka-DOSH	קָדוֹשׁ	B3
instruction (Word of GOD)	*fs*	to-RA	תּוֹרָה	B4
LORD** (see C2)	*ms*	a-do-NAI	יְהוָה	B5
name	*ms*	shem	שֵׁם	B6
peace, hello, goodbye	*ms*	sha-LOM	שָׁלוֹם	B7
Sabbath	*fs*	sha-BAT	שַׁבָּת	B8

*Most Hebrew nouns and verbs have genders and numbers.   B9
(ms=masculine singular, fs=feminine singular, mpl=masculine plural, fpl=feminine plural)
For more information on plurals, see Lesson 4.

C – Pronunciation

Look at the transliteration column in the vocabulary list above. As you learn the new   C1
words, this transliteration chart below will help you pronounce them.

a	"a" as in <u>a</u>ll	kh	"ch" as in Ba<u>ch</u>
e	"e" as in <u>e</u>nter	ay	"ay" as is l<u>ay</u>
ee	"ee" as in f<u>ee</u>t	ai	"i" as in p<u>ie</u>
o	"o" as in <u>o</u>ver	oy	"oy" as in b<u>oy</u>
oo	"oo" as in t<u>oo</u>	ooey	"ooey" as in g<u>ooey</u>

CAPITAL letters show the accented syllable in a word as in "sha-LOM"
If the accent is *not* on the last syllable, it will be **BOLD** as in "**ME**-lekh"

**Pronouncing יְהוָה C2

יְהוָה, ("LORD" in English) is the "unpronounceable name of אֱלֹהִים." It is used over 6000 times in the Scriptures! In this course, I have chosen to use the word "ADONAI" (literally "my master") when pronouncing יְהוָה. Other names include (but are not limited to) "Yahweh," "Yehovah," "Yah," and "HaShem." Please use the name you are comfortable with.

Sephardic Pronunciation

Throughout *Hebrew with Joy! in the Biblical Feasts,* we will use the **Sephardic** pronunciation to honor the Hebrew pronunciation used in Israel.

Examples		Origin	Accent	Name	
to-RA sha-BAT	תּוֹרָה שַׁבָּת	Israel, Middle East, Spain, Portugal, North Africa	Accent is usually on the **LAST** syllable.	**Sephardic**	C3
TO-ra **SHA**-bas	תּוֹרָה שַׁבָּת	France, Germany, Eastern Europe (origin of most Jewish Americans)	Accent is usually on the **FIRST** syllable.	**Ashkenazi**	C4

Tip: Pronouncing Biblical Names   C5

Israeli Hebrew teacher, Rivka Simms, shares this עִבְרִית tip: Almost all עִבְרִית names found in the Scriptures are accented on the last syllable. For example,

Abraham אַבְרָהָם (av-ra-HAM)   Isaac יִצְחָק (yeets-KHAK)

Jacob יַעֲקֹב (ya-a-KOV)   Moses מֹשֶׁה (mo-SHE)

Cantillation Marks   C6

Along with the Hebrew vowels, you will notice there are other markings in Biblical עִבְרִית called **cantillation marks**. They are used to divide verses into smaller units of meaning and have musical value, allowing Cantors (song leaders) to chant the verses. <u>These marks are helpful as they also show the accented syllable of each word!</u>
(*Notice the accent marks circled in the Scripture from Psalm 119:18 below.*)

C7   גַּל־עֵינַי וְאַבִּיטָה נִפְלָאוֹת מִתּוֹרָתֶךָ:

mee-to-ra-**TE**-kha	neef-la-OT	v-a-**BEE**-ta	ay-NAI	gal
from your instruction	*wonders*	*and (I will) behold*	*my eyes*	*open*

This is one of my favorite Scriptures, and I encourage you to recite it before you study   C8

the _____ of _____.
        instruction*   LORD*

*The answers to the Fill-Ins are found in Appendix D   C9

D – Roots

From the root of one tree, come many similar branches, each different and unique.   **D1**
עִבְרִית roots are the same! From each root come many words that share similar meanings.

Root meaning rest, stop	שׁ.ב.ת Used 172 X in the Scriptures!	Most roots are built from three letters.	D2
		Middle and bottom dots and vowels are not written in roots. (Note: In this book, periods are used between the letters of the root.)	D3
	שַׁבָּת	Words from the same root share similar meanings. Extra letters, different vowels, prefixes, and suffixes change the meaning.	D4
Sabbaths	שַׁבָּתוֹת		
to sit	לָשֶׁבֶת		
to rest	לִשְׁבּוֹת		
Sabbatical	שַׁבָּתוֹן		

Fill in the missing English word above. (<u>The Fill-In answers are in Appendix D</u>)   **D5**
In the Hebrew words above, circle the root letters meaning to "rest" or "stop."

A complete list of the roots included in this book is in Appendix E.   **D6**

Look at the root of שָׁלוֹם. Fill in the missing word, then circle the root letters in each word.   D7

Words from the Root		Root Meaning	Root
	peace, hello, goodbye	completion, wholeness	שׁ.ל.ם used 236 X in the Scriptures
שָׁלֵם	whole, complete		
שְׁלֵמוּת	perfection		
שְׁלֹמֹה	Solomon		
יְרוּשָׁלַיִם	Jerusalem		

---

*"**Jerusalem**" (y-roo-sha-**LAI**-yeem in Hebrew) comes from the root* שׁ.ל.ם   D8
        y-roo= they will see (one possible meaning)
        sha-lem = peace, wholeness, completion, and perfection
        *sha-**LAI**-yeem= "**LAI**-yeem" ending means <u>double</u> shalom!*

שֵׁם_____   1 - Moving Forward Exercises

Read and translate the following words.   1.

קָדוֹשׁ   שַׁבָּת   תּוֹרָה   שֵׁם   שָׁלוֹם   אֱלֹהִים   עִבְרִית   יְהוָה

Fill in the missing words and their translations below. (Don't forget the vowels!)   2.

Hebrew	English	Hebrew	English
עִבְרִית		יְהוָה	LORD
	instruction	אֱלֹהִים	
	Sabbath		holy
שֵׁם			peace, hello, goodbye

Most roots are built from how many letters? _____   3.

Write three Hebrew words (and their English meanings) that come from the root שׁ.ב.ת.   4.

_____   _____   _____   English

_____   _____   _____   Hebrew

_____ What is the root meaning of שׁ.ל.ם?   5.

_____ Which syllable is usually accented in the Sephardic style?   6.

_____ Why are cantillation marks helpful?   7.

_____

What do you know NOW?

Match the answers below that you know already. Don't look up any answers.

PLEASE LEAVE THE ANSWERS BLANK THAT YOU DON'T KNOW!

At the end of class, you'll take a similar quiz to see what you have learned.

2. Match the roots to their meaning.

completion, wholeness ____	שׁ.א.ר	A
joyful, rejoice ____	שׁ.ד.ח	B
cover, protect ____	שׁ.ל.ם	C
hide, conceal ____	ס.ת.ר	D
seven ____	י.ד.ה	E
head, beginning ____	שׁ.מ.ח	F
new, renew ____	שׁ.ב.ע	G
praise, give thanks ____	א.מ.ן	H
truly ____	מ.ל.ך	I
rule, reign ____	כ.פ.ר	J
rest, stop ____	שׁ.ב.ת	K

1. Match the words to their meaning.

head ____	קָצִיר	A
LORD ____	יְהוָה	B
Hebrew ____	שִׂמְחָה	C
leaven ____	מְלָאכָה	D
Jews ____	רֹאשׁ	E
joy ____	עָנָה	F
holiday ____	עִבְרִית	G
afflict, deny ____	פְּרִי	H
harvest ____	חָמֵץ	I
fruit ____	יְהוּדִים	J
work ____	חַג	K

4. Match the holidays to their meaning.

Day of the Atonements ____	סֻכּוֹת	A
First Fruits ____	שָׁבוּעוֹת	B
Day of the Blasting ____	יוֹם הַכִּפֻּרִים	C
Feast of Weeks ____	הַמַּצּוֹת	D
Feast of Dedication ____	יוֹם תְּרוּעָה	E
Feast of Booths ____	פֶּסַח	F
Feast of Lots ____	פּוּרִים	G
Sabbath ____	חֲנֻכָּה	H
Unleavened Bread ____	שַׁבָּת	I
Passover ____	בִּיכּוּרִים	J

3. Match the words to their meaning.

seven ____	אוֹר	A
appointed times ____	מֶלֶך	B
good ____	מוֹעֲדִים	C
salvation ____	יְשׁוּעָה	D
holy, holiness ____	חֹדֶשׁ	E
fast ____	צוֹם	F
light ____	שֶׁבַע	G
year ____	קֹדֶשׁ	H
days ____	שָׁנָה	I
month ____	טוֹב	J
king ____	יָמִים	K

2 – GOD's Appointed Times מוֹעֲדִים

> **Holiday Greeting**
> Happy Holiday!　　חַג שָׂמֵחַ!

A – Vocabulary

Memorize the following Hebrew words used in this lesson.

English	Gender	Transliteration	Hebrew	
appointed time	ms	mo-ED	מוֹעֵד	A1
appointed times	mpl	mo-a-DEEM	מוֹעֲדִים	A2
blessed	ms	ba-ROOKH	בָּרוּךְ	A3
convocation	ms	meek-RA	מִקְרָא	A4
happy, rejoicing	ms	sa-**ME**-akh	שָׂמֵחַ	A5
holiday, feast	ms	khag	חַג	A6
holidays, feasts	mpl	kha-GEEM	חַגִּים	A7
holiness (noun)	ms	**KO**-desh	קֹדֶשׁ	A8
Israel	fs	yees-ra-EL	יִשְׂרָאֵל	A9
king	ms	**ME**-lekh	מֶלֶךְ	A10

A11

> *The* מוֹעֲדִים *of* יְהוָה *can be called* חַגִּים *(kha-GEEM) meaning "_____" but can also mean "to revolve around." The Biblical cycle of* מוֹעֲדִים *is a never-ending circle that keeps revolving around year after year after year - a pattern which gives life a _____ rhythm.*
> Hannah Nesher, VoiceforIsrael.com　　holy

B - מוֹעֲדִים Scriptures

It is a joy and delight to meet with our Holy יְהוָה on His calendar, at His appointed times. **B1**
They are to be eternal reminders of His faithfulness to us.

Leviticus 23:1-2 *Then ADONAI spoke to Moses saying: "Speak to the children of* יִשְׂרָאֵל **B2**
and tell them: These are the מוֹעֲדִים *of* יְהוָה*, which you are to proclaim to be convocations of* קֹדֶשׁ *—My* מוֹעֲדִים*."*

Numbers 10:10 *"Also at your days of rejoicing,* מוֹעֲדִים *and new moons, you are to blow* **B3**
on the trumpets over your burnt offerings and fellowship offerings. They will then be a reminder for you before יְהוָה *your God. I am* יְהוָה *your God!"*

From Leviticus 23:2, fill in the missing English words: B4

אֹתָם	תִּקְרְאוּ	אֲשֶׁר־	יְהוָה	*מוֹעֲדֵי	וַיְקְרָא 23:2
them	you (are to) proclaim	which		_____ _____ (of)	Leviticus 23:2

מוֹעֲדָי	הֵם	אֵלֶּה	קֹדֶשׁ	*מִקְרָאֵי
_____ _____ My	them	these (are)		_____ (of)

These endings will be discussed in Lesson 8

Did you notice that certain English words are assumed in עִבְרִית? B5
The words "is," "am," "are," and sometimes "of" do not translate into Hebrew.
Notice the examples in the תּוֹרָה Scripture above.

C – Which מוֹעֲדִים will we study?

In this book, we will have a lesson for each of the מוֹעֲדִים included in Leviticus 23. C1
These special "GOD appointments" include: Sabbath, Passover, Unleavened Bread
(included in the Passover lesson), Feast of Weeks, Day of Blasting, Day of
Atonements, and Feast of Booths (including the Joy of Torah).
*To see a summary of these מוֹעֲדִים, refer to Appendix M.

We've also included these beloved חַגִּים:
Feast of Lots (from the book of Esther) and the Feast of Dedication.

Translate these מוֹעֲדִים and חַגִּים into English:
(If you need help, refer to the Dictionary in Appendix L.)

שָׁבוּעוֹת	פֶּסַח	פּוּרִים	סֻכּוֹת	שַׁבָּת	C2
_____	_____	_____	_____	_____	
_____	_____	_____	_____	_____	

חֲנֻכָּה	הַמַּצּוֹת	יוֹם הַכִּפֻּרִים	יוֹם תְּרוּעָה	C3
_____	_____	_____	_____	
_____	_____	_____	_____	

D – Syllable Lines

A helpful way to pronounce a new word (especially a long one!) is to break it into syllables first, then pronounce each syllable.   D1

הַ | כִּ | פֻּ | רִים

Note on Shva vowels: If the Shvah **:** occurs under the first letter of a word, it has a short "uh" sound. In the middle of the word, it is <u>usually</u> silent and ends the syllable. At the end of the word, it is always silent.   D2

Each syllable will have only ONE sounded vowel.   D3

תְּ | רוּ | עָה   מִקְ | רָא

a   ROO   tuh   RA   meek

If the Shva is silent as in מִקְרָא, it does not count as a sounded vowel and it ends the syllable. If the Shva has a sound as in תְּרוּעָה, it counts as a sounded vowel.   D4

To practice, draw syllable lines in the עִבְרִית words in section E1 below. Then pronounce each word out loud.   D5

E – Hebrew Root מ.ל.ך

Fill in the missing word, then circle the root letters in the עִבְרִית words below.

Words from the Root		Root Meaning	Root	
king				
queen	מַלְכָּה			
kingdom	מַלְכוּת	rule, reign	מ.ל.ך used 2523X In the Scriptures!	E1
our king	מַלְכֵּנוּ			
to reign	לִמְלוֹךְ			

During each מוֹעֵד, we have the honor of meeting with our glorious מֶלֶךְ!   E2

F – Pilgrimage to Jerusalem

F1

Three times a year!

Exodus 23:14 *"Three times in the year you are to celebrate a festival for Me…"*

The "three times" included enough days to ensure that all Hebrew men would

be in Jerusalem for the following yearly מוֹעֲדִים found in Leviticus 23:

Spring: הַמַּצּוֹת   Summer: שָׁבוּעוֹת   Fall: סֻכּוֹת

There were two special עִבְרִית names for this mitzvah (command):

1) As a corporate group, the journey was called שָׁלוֹשׁ רְגָלִים "sha-LOSH rag-**LAI**-yeem" (three legs): <u>three</u> times a year the men would walk by <u>foot</u> to celebrate in Jerusalem.

2) For an individual, this pilgrimage trip was called עֲלִיָּיה לְרֶגֶל "a-lee-YA l-**RE**-gel" (going <u>up</u> by foot) because one must walk "up" the mountain to Jerusalem.

G – Holiday Greeting In Israel

We learned the standard holiday greeting at the beginning of this lesson. However, in   G1
Israel, it is customary to add the name of the holiday between "khag" and "sa-**ME**-akh."

חַג _(holiday name)_ שָׂמֵחַ!

In Hebrew the adjective comes after the noun it describes.   G2
So our חַג שָׂמֵחַ literally translates to "Holiday happy!"

Read and translate the following greetings into English.   G3

חַג סֻכּוֹת שָׂמֵחַ!

_____

חַג פֶּסַח שָׂמֵחַ!

_____

חַג חֲנֻכָּה שָׂמֵחַ!

_____

How would you write in עִבְרִית "Happy Feast of Weeks holiday?"   G4

_____   _____   _____

You can learn more about Hebrew adjectives in *Biblical Hebrew with Joy!* Lesson 10.   G5

H - She-he-khe-**YA**-noo שֶׁהֶחֱיָנוּ Prayer

Birth of a Nation

On May 14, 1948, David Ben Gurion read the Israeli Declaration of Independence, Rabbi Yehuda Maimon prayed the Shehecheyanu prayer, then the declaration was signed. At that moment, the State of Israel was born.

H1

For 2000 years, the שֶׁהֶחֱיָנוּ (she-he-khe-**YA**-noo) "who has kept us alive" prayer has been recited during each of the מוֹעֲדִים of יְהוָה. It expresses gratitude to יְהוָה for His goodness in allowing us to experience each מוֹעֵד once again.

H2

Listen to the prayer below on the Lesson 2 audio file or use the QR code (on left) to view the WTS Hebrew Players using sign language (https://youtu.be/1eVcR-Zih4s).

H3

הָעוֹלָם	מֶלֶךְ	אֱלֹהֵינוּ	יְהוָה	אַתָּה	בָּרוּךְ
the universe	king	our GOD	LORD	You	blessed

הַזֶּה	לַזְּמַן	וְהִגִּיעָנוּ	וְקִיְּמָנוּ	שֶׁהֶחֱיָנוּ
ha-ZEH	laz-MAN	v-hee-gee-**A**-noo	v-kee-**MA**-noo	she-he-khe-**YA**-noo
this	to time	and brought us	and sustained us	kept us alive

Blessed (are) You, LORD our GOD, King (of) the universe,
who has kept us alive, and sustained us and brought us to this
season (time).

The "נוּ" Ending

Did you notice that four words in the שֶׁהֶחֱיָנוּ prayer end with the "נוּ" ending? In עִבְרִית, the "נוּ" ending means "we," "us" or "our." The Scriptures are full of Hebrew words ending in "נוּ". For example, Isaiah 7:14 tells us: "Behold, the virgin will conceive. When she is giving birth to a son, she will call his name <u>Immanuel</u>."

<u>Immanuel</u> comes from two Hebrew words אֵל   עִמָּ+נוּ

GOD   us   with

עִבְרִית Tip: In most cases, the syllable right before the "נוּ" ending will be the accented syllable!

*You can learn more about עִבְרִית word endings (suffixes) in *Biblical Hebrew with Joy!* Lessons 5, 8 & 9.

H4

I – Monthly מוֹעֵד

Rosh KHO-desh

I1

"At your days of rejoicing, מוֹעֲדִים *and **new moons**, you are to blow on the trumpets over your burnt offerings and fellowship offerings. They will then be a reminder for you before* יְהוָֹה *your God. I am* יְהוָֹה *your God!"* (Numbers 10:10)

In Numbers 10:10, יְהוָֹה commands us to remember the מוֹעֲדִים and each "New Moon" (rosh **KHO**-desh). The Hebrew (רֹאשׁ חֹדֶשׁ) literally translates to "head of the month," as each new עִבְרִית month begins with the first sighting of the sliver of the new moon.

How can you celebrate רֹאשׁ חֹדֶשׁ? When you sight the new moon, bring an offering and blow the shofar to bring a sacrifice of praise to _____!
LORD

Why Study the מוֹעֲדִים?

I2

"To understand the Feasts - the symbolism, the rituals, the when and the whys, the customs, the traditions - will open up a whole new dimension of understanding. There's just something extraordinary and awe-inspiring in knowing the מוֹעֲדִים *were directly ordained by* יְהוָֹה *and that He had specific reasons for doing so."*
Teresa Douglas, Tennessee

---

2 - God's Appointed Times
Exercises

שֵׁם _____

1. Be ready to and translate the following עִבְרִית words.

מוֹעֲדִים שָׁלוֹם שָׂמֵחַ קָדוֹשׁ מִקְרָא אֱלֹהִים קֹדֶשׁ
חַג תּוֹרָה מוֹעֵד שַׁבָּת בָּרוּךְ מֶלֶךְ עִבְרִית שֵׁם

Look up the following scriptures from Leviticus 23 and write the name in עִבְרִית for each מוֹעֵד.

2. 3 "Work may be done for six days, but the seventh day is a _____ of solemn rest, a holy convocation. "

3. 5 "During the first month, on the fourteenth day of the month in the evening, is Adonai's _____."

4. 24 "Speak to Bnei-Yisrael, saying: In the seventh month, on the first day of the month, you are to have a Shabbat rest, a memorial of _____ , a holy convocation."

5. 27 "However, the tenth day of this seventh month is _____ _____ a holy convocation to you, so you are to afflict yourselves."

6. 34 "Speak to Bnei-Yisrael, and say, "On the fifteenth day of this seventh month is _____ , for seven days to Adonai."

7. (from Deuteronomy 16:9)
"Seven weeks you are to count for yourself—from the time you begin to put the sickle to the standing grain you will begin to count seven _____."

8. For the following Hebrew words, draw syllable lines, then write the English translation below.

שָׂמֵחַ	מוֹעֲדִים	שָׁבוּעוֹת	Hebrew
			English

23

9.   Write in Hebrew: "Happy Passover Holiday":

_____   _____   _____

10.   What is the meaning of the root מ.ל.ך ?

_____

11.   Write (in Hebrew) two words that comes from this root, then write the English meanings:

_____H   _____H

_____E   _____E

12.   In your own words, explain why the מוֹעֲדִים are important:

_____

_____

_____

_____

_____

_____

_____

_____

_____

_____

3 - Sabbath שַׁבָּת

Greeting: Sabbath (of) Peace שַׁבָּת שָׁלוֹם!

A – Vocabulary

Memorize the following Hebrew words used in this lesson:

English	Gender	Transliteration	Hebrew	
blessing	fs	b-ra-KHA	בְּרָכָה	A1
day	ms	yom	יוֹם	A2
days	mpl	ya-MEEM	יָמִים	A3
delight	ms	**O**-neg	עֹנֶג	A4
evening	ms	**E**-rev	עֶרֶב	A5
observe/guard/keep	ms	sha-MOR	שָׁמוֹר	A6
remember	ms	za-KHOR	זָכוֹר	A7
so be it	-	a-MEN	אָמֵן	A8
universe/world/forever	ms	o-LAM	עוֹלָם	A9
work (occupation/employment)	fs	m-la-KHA	מְלָאכָה	A10

A10

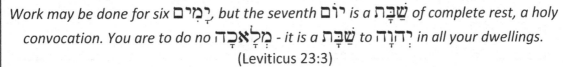

Why Celebrate שַׁבָּת?

Work may be done for six יָמִים, but the seventh יוֹם is a שַׁבָּת of complete rest, a holy convocation. You are to do no מְלָאכָה - it is a שַׁבָּת to יְהוָה in all your dwellings.
(Leviticus 23:3)

In Leviticus 23, Adonai's first מוֹעֵד is the שַׁבָּת. It is a divine appointment with יְהוָה, created for our goodness, health, and blessing. שַׁבָּת is a "sanctuary of קָדוֹשׁ time" in which we separate ourselves from the "ordinary" and focus on the "holiness" of יְהוָה. It is our time to spend with our Heavenly Father as we "unplug" from the worldly stresses and challenges of the week and become "set apart" for Him!

שַׁבָּת is a sign between יְהוָה and His people that we are no longer slaves in Egypt, but that יְהוָה has set us free! Hallelujah and אָמֵן!

B – שַׁבָּת Scriptures

As we learned in Lesson 1, שַׁבָּת is found 172 times in the Word of אֱלֹהִים and the root, שׁ.ב.ת means to "rest" or "stop." What do the Scriptures below show about the heart of יְהוָה for שַׁבָּת? **B1**

Genesis 2:1-3 *"So the heavens and the earth were completed along with their entire array.* אֱלֹהִים *completed on the seventh* יוֹם *His work "m-lakh-TO"* (מְלַאכְתּוֹ*) *that He made, and He ceased on the seventh* יוֹם *from all* מְלַאכְתּוֹ* *that He made. Then* אֱלֹהִים *blessed the seventh* יוֹם *and sanctified it, for on it He ceased from all* מְלַאכְתּוֹ* *that* אֱלֹהִים *created for the purpose of preparing."* **B2**

*Biblical Hebrew often adds possessive pronouns as suffixes (endings). Example above - מְלַאכְתּוֹ (<u>His</u> work). You can learn more about suffixes in *Biblical Hebrew with Joy!* Lessons 5, 8 & 9. **B3**

Exodus 31:13,16 *"Speak now to the children of* יִשְׂרָאֵל *saying, 'Surely you must keep My Sabbaths, for it is a <u>sign</u> between Me and you throughout your generations, so you may know that I am* יְהוָה *who sanctifies you'… So, the children of* יִשְׂרָאֵל *are to keep the* שַׁבָּת, *to* שָׁמוֹר *the* שַׁבָּת *throughout their generations as a perpetual covenant."* **B4**

B5

Ancient שַׁבָּת

From the Scripture above, the ancient Paleo script paints an amazing picture:

ת	ב	שׁ	←Letter
†	⊡	⊔	←Ancient Picture
covenant/sign	house/tent	chew/press	←Meaning

On שַׁבָּת, we are to "press home" to the "covenant" with יְהוָה.

Isaiah 58:13-14 *"If you turn back your foot from* שַׁבָּת, *from doing your pleasure on My holy* יוֹם, *and call* _____ *an* עֹנֶג, *the holy* יוֹם *of* יְהוָה *honorable, if you honor it, not* **B6**
Sabbath
going your own ways, not seeking your own pleasure, nor speaking your usual speech, then you will delight yourself in יְהוָה, *and I will let you ride over the heights of the earth, I will feed you with the heritage of your father Jacob." For the mouth of* _____ *has spoken.*
LORD

In the previous section, we read the specific commands of יְהֹוָה to observe שַׁבָּת. Did you   B7
realize that remembering the שַׁבָּת is even one of the 10 Commandments? עֲשֶׂרֶת הַדְּבָרִים
(a-SE-ret ha-d-va-REEM) - literally "The Ten Words." Fill in the missing English and Hebrew words.

לְקַדְּשׁוֹ	הַשַּׁבָּת		אֶת־*		שְׁמוֹת 20:8(7)	B8
to keep it holy (to holy it)	the	day	---	remember	Exodus 20:8(7)	

* אֶת does not translate into English but is a pointer to the word which follows it, which   B9
is the **specific** direct object of the sentence.

Now it is time to practice writing your Hebrew! The Scripture below is almost the same
as Exodus 20:8 above. Only one word is different! Fill in the missing words.

			אֶת־		דְּבָרִים 5:12(11)	B10
to keep it holy	the Sabbath	day	---	observe/ guard/keep	Deuteronomy 5:12(11)	

C – Prefixes

As you have seen, one Hebrew word is often translated into many English words.   C1
Did you notice the prefix at the beginning of the word הַשַּׁבָּת?

הַ + שַׁבָּת
the   Sabbath

Now, take a look at the word לְקַדְּשׁוֹ, which includes a prefix at the beginning   C2
and also a suffix at the end!

לְ + קַדְּשׁ + וֹ
to/for   holy   it (ms)

In English, we need four words to say "to keep it holy" but in Hebrew it is combined
into just one word which literally means "to holy it!"

Read the following words with prefixes, then write the English meaning below each one.   C3

לְיִשְׂרָאֵל	הַיָּמִים	לְקַדְּשׁוֹ	הָעֶרֶב	הַבְּרָכָה
_____	_____	_____	_____	_____

You can learn more about prefixes in *Biblical Hebrew with Joy!* Lessons 3 & 4.   C4

D –The Blessing of GOD בְּרָכָה

The following blessing begins many Hebrew prayers and is sometimes called the בְּרָכָה **D1**
(blessing) "The Blessing of GOD." If you have not already memorized this בְּרָכָה, take some
time right now to begin! I find it easier to memorize if the words are set to music.
To hear the Shabbat prayers, go to: hebrewwithjoy.com/hjbf-audios/

הָעוֹלָם	מֶלֶךְ	אֱלֹהֵינוּ	יְהוָה	אַתָּה	בָּרוּךְ	**D2**
ha-o-LAM	**ME**-lekh	e-lo-**HAY**-noo	a-do-NAI	a-TA	ba-ROOKH	
the universe	king (of)	our GOD	LORD	You	blessed (are)	

Remember that certain English words are assumed in עִבְרִית. **D3**
The words "is," "am," "are," and sometimes "of" do not translate into עִבְרִית.
Notice the examples of "are" and "of" in the עִבְרִית blessing above.

 # E - Prayer of Sanctification - קִדּוּשׁ

The special בְּרָכָה over the wine is called the קִדּוּשׁ (kee-DOOSH), which means **E1**
"sanctification." So, as this בְּרָכָה is recited around the world every עֶרֶב שַׁבָּת, each
family is sanctifying the שַׁבָּת as קָדוֹשׁ, sacred and set apart. Even the special meal is called
an עֹנֶג which means_____. Celebrating the שַׁבָּת is truly a delight!

Refer to D2 above and write the missing words below from the קִדּוּשׁ.

הָעוֹלָם		אֱלֹהֵינוּ		אַתָּה		Hebrew	**E2**
____	King (of)	____	LORD	____	blessed (are)	English	

אָמֵן	הַגֶּפֶן	פְּרִי	בּוֹרֵא	Hebrew
	____ vine	fruit (of)	creator (of)	English

F – שַׁבָּת Traditions

Weekly Preparation in יִשְׂרָאֵל   F1

In יִשְׂרָאֵל, the work week is Sunday through Friday. (Yes, Israelis work on Sundays!) In fact, most Israeli businesses, restaurants and malls are closed by noon on Fridays! Before שַׁבָּת, each week, the preparations begin – the house is cleaned, the groceries and fresh flowers are purchased, the Challah (braided bread) is baked, and the table is set with the very best. Now, שַׁבָּת can begin!

Candle-Lighting   F2

For centuries, the lighting of candles to welcome in שַׁבָּת has occurred before sundown on Friday עֶרֶב. In fact, Biblical calendars include candle-lighting times, 18 minutes before the actual sunset to make sure that the candles are not lit after the שַׁבָּת begins. Why? The answer comes from Exodus 35:3: *"Do not kindle a fire in any of your dwellings on יוֹם הַשַׁבָּת."*

After the mother of the home lights the candles, she closes her eyes and circles the candles three times with her hands - a beautiful tradition symbolizing that we are to push away the "ordinary" and "common" of the week and draw in the "sacredness" and "holiness" of שַׁבָּת.

Traditionally, two candles are lit, but in some homes, the mother lights additional candles for each family member. What do two candles symbolize? Answers vary but most agree that we are to both "זָכוֹר" and "שָׁמוֹר" the שַׁבָּת. Another beautiful reason is that יְהוָה is both our "Creator" and our "Redeemer."

Two Loaves of Bread   F3

Although most families pray a בְּרָכָה over a loaf of bread before their meal every day, on עֶרֶב שַׁבָּת, they pray over two loaves of challah. Why? When יְהוָה rained down manna in the wilderness, He commanded the Children of Israel to pick up a double portion on the 6th day, so they would not work on שַׁבָּת.

Family Blessings   F4

One of my favorite שַׁבָּת traditions is the blessing of each family member. What an amazing way to affirm each person on a weekly basis! Traditionally, the parents bless the children and one another. The mothers are even blessed with Proverbs 31! In our challenging world today, full of so much negativity, don't we all want and need a blessing in our lives?

Havdalah הַבְדָּלָה – "Separating" from Shabbat   F5

This is a beautiful ritual that is celebrated at the end of Shabbat, when the first three stars are sighted in the sky on Saturday evening. A special twisted candle is lit, a cup of wine is filled to overflowing (as our שַׁבָּת joy has filled us to overflowing), and a fragrant box of spices is passed around symbolizing the sweetness of שַׁבָּת.

G – Hebrew Root א.מ.ן

G1

אָמֵן

Have you noticed that most Hebrew prayers end with the word אָמֵן "Amen?" Even though this is a Hebrew word, it has become so popular, it is a part of the English dictionary! But אָמֵן does not only end a prayer, its root shows also that it is a strong and powerful way of saying, "*Yes, I believe in faith, this is truth!*"
Look at the Hebrew words below that come from this incredible root!

In the chart below, fill in the blank then circle the root letters in the Hebrew words.

Words from the Root		Root Meaning	Root	
so be it			א.מ.ן	G2
faith	אֱמוּנָה	truly	used 138X	
truth	אֱמֶת		In the Scriptures	
believe	מַאֲמִין			

H- Personal שַׁבָּת Prayer

One way to memorize new vocabulary is to write it as often as possible. The prayer below uses much of the Hebrew vocabulary for this lesson. Write the missing Hebrew words on the lines below, then read it <u>out loud</u> as a בְּרָכָה to יְהוָה:

Dear _____, Thank You for _____ _____.
      LORD   day   the Sabbath

You commanded us: _____ it! _____ it! Help me
                      remember   observe/guard/keep

_____. May it be an _____ to You. _____
  to keep it holy   delight   so be it!

I – Sabbath שַׁבָּת Guide

If you've never celebrated שַׁבָּת, the שַׁבָּת Guide on the next two pages could be a helpful starting point. It can be downloaded at hebrewwithjoy.com/hjbf-book-handouts/.
Please feel free to add or change any part of the Guide as you feel led!

Sabbath שַׁבָּת Guide

Exodus 20:8-11(7-10) "Remember Yom ha-Shabbat [day of the Sabbath] to keep it holy. You are to work six days, and do all your work, but the seventh day is a Shabbat to Adonai (the LORD) your God. In it you shall not do any work… For in six days Adonai made heaven and earth, the sea, and all that is in them, and rested on the seventh day. Thus Adonai blessed Yom Shabbat, and made it holy."

Isaiah 58:13-14 "If you turn back your foot from Shabbat, from doing your pleasure on My holy day, and call Shabbat a delight, the holy day of Adonai honorable, if you honor it, not going your own ways, not seeking your own pleasure, nor speaking your usual speech, then You will delight yourself in Adonai, and I will let you ride over the heights of the earth. I will feed you with the heritage of your father Jacob."

 ## Candle Lighting בְּרָכָה
(new prayer from Exodus 20:8)

בָּרוּךְ אַתָּה יְהוָה אֱלֹהֵינוּ מֶלֶךְ הָעוֹלָם
אֲשֶׁר צִוָּנוּ לְכַבֵּד אֶת הַשַׁבָּת וּלְקַדְשָׁהּ. אָמֵן

ba-ROOKH a-TA a-do-NAI, e-lo-**HAY**-noo **ME**-lekh ha-o-LAM,
a-SHER tsee-**VA**-noo l-kha-BED et ha-sha-BAT ool-kad-SHA. *a-MEN*

We praise You, LORD our GOD, King of the universe,
who has commanded us to honor the Sabbath and to keep it holy. Amen

הַמּוֹצִיא (Who Brings Forth) - בְּרָכָה for the Giver of the Bread

בָּרוּךְ אַתָּה יְהוָה אֱלֹהֵינוּ מֶלֶךְ הָעוֹלָם הַמּוֹצִיא לֶחֶם מִן הָאָרֶץ. אָמֵן

ba-ROOKH a-TA a-do-NAI, e-lo-**HAY**-noo **ME**-lekh ha-o-LAM, ha-**MO**-tsee **LE**-khem meen ha-**A**-rets. a-MEN
Blessed are You, LORD our GOD, Ruler of the universe, who brings forth bread from the earth. Amen

קִדּוּשׁ (Sanctification) - בְּרָכָה for the Giver of the Fruit of the Vine

בָּרוּךְ אַתָּה יְהוָה אֱלֹהֵינוּ מֶלֶךְ הָעוֹלָם בּוֹרֵא פְּרִי הַגָּפֶן. אָמֵן.

ba-ROOKH a-TA a-do-NAI, e-lo-**HAY**-noo **ME**-lekh ha-o-LAM, bo-RE p-REE ha-**GA**-fen. *a-MEN*
Blessed are you, LORD our GOD, Ruler of the universe, who creates the fruit of the vine. Amen

שְׁמַע

שְׁמַע יִשְׂרָאֵל יְהוָה אֱלֹהֵינוּ יְהוָה אֶחָד:
בָּרוּךְ שֵׁם כְּבוֹד מַלְכוּתוֹ לְעוֹלָם וָעֶד:

sh-MA yees-ra-EL a-do-NAI e-lo-**HAY**-noo a-do-NAI e-KHAD:
ba-ROOKH shem k-VOD mal-**KHOO**-to l-o-LAM va-ED.

Hear (O) Israel, the LORD our God, the LORD is one.
Blessed is the name of His glorious kingdom for ever and ever.

Family Blessings

For Sons

May Adonai inspire you to love in the tradition of Abraham, Isaac and Jacob.
May you grow closer to Adonai, our LORD, in strength and dignity and shine His light to those around you!

For Daughters

May Adonai inspire you to love in the tradition of Sarah and Rebekah, Rachel and Leah.
May you grow in the love of Adonai, our King, and be a light to the world!

Blessing the Parents (by the children)

May GOD bless your love for one another and for us!

For the Wife (adapted from Proverbs 31)

A woman of valor – who can find? She is to be valued above rubies. Her husband trusts in her, and so he lacks nothing. She does him good, never harm, all the days of her life. She reached out to those in need, and extends her hands to the poor. She is clothed in strength and dignity and she faces the future cheerfully. She speaks with wisdom; the law of kindness is on her lips. She shines with the love of Adonai to her family and in her community. Her children rise up and bless her; her husband sings her praises.

For the Husband (adapted from Psalm 112)

Blessed is the man who fears and glorifies Adonai, who greatly delights in Adonai's commandments. The generation of the upright will be blessed. His household prospers, and his righteousness endures forever. Light shines in the darkness for the upright. For the one who is gracious, compassionate and just. He is not afraid of evil tidings; his mind is firm; trusting in Adonai. His heart is steady, he will not be afraid. He gives freely to the poor. His righteousness endures forever; his life is exalted in honor.

The Aaronic בְּרָכָה

יְבָרֶכְךָ יְהוָה וְיִשְׁמְרֶךָ: יָאֵר יְהוָה פָּנָיו אֵלֶיךָ וִיחֻנֶּךָ:
יִשָּׂא יְהוָה פָּנָיו אֵלֶיךָ וְיָשֵׂם לְךָ שָׁלוֹם:

y-va-re-kh-KHA a-do-NAI v-yeesh-m-**RE**-kha; ya-ER a-do-NAI pa-NAV e-**LE**-kha vee-khoo-**NE**-kha;
yee-SA a-do-NAI pa-NAV e-**LE**-kha v-ya-SEM l-KHA sha-LOM
Adonai bless you and keep you! Adonai make His face to shine on you and be gracious to you!
Adonai turn his face to you and grant you shalom. Numbers 6:24-26

שַׁבָּת שָׁלוֹם!

3 - Sabbath Exercises

שֵׁם _____

.1 Read and be able to translate the following Hebrew words.

שָׁמוֹר   מוֹעֲדִים   מִקְרָא   זָכוֹר   עֹנֶג   שָׂמַח   קֹדֶשׁ

לְקַדְּשׁוֹ   יִשְׂרָאֵל   עֶרֶב   מוֹעֵד   תּוֹרָה   מְלָאכָה   יוֹם

.2 In the following Scripture, Isaiah 58:13-14 (circle) the Hebrew for the following words/roots.

Sabbath (2X), day, delight (2X), LORD (3X)

(Remember the words could have a prefix and/or a suffix attached.)

אִם־תָּשִׁיב מִשַּׁבָּת רַגְלֶךָ עֲשׂוֹת חֲפָצֶיךָ בְּיוֹם קָדְשִׁי וְקָרָאתָ לַשַּׁבָּת עֹנֶג לִקְדוֹשׁ יְהוָה מְכֻבָּד וְכִבַּדְתּוֹ מֵעֲשׂוֹת דְּרָכֶיךָ מִמְּצוֹא חֶפְצְךָ וְדַבֵּר דָּבָר:

אָז תִּתְעַנַּג עַל־יְהוָה וְהִרְכַּבְתִּיךָ עַל־בָּמוֹתֵי "עַל־בָּמֳתֵי" אָרֶץ וְהַאֲכַלְתִּיךָ נַחֲלַת יַעֲקֹב אָבִיךָ כִּי פִּי יְהוָה דִּבֵּר: ס

.3 What is the meaning of the prefix לְ? _____

.4 What is the English meaning of the following words?

לַיהוָה   הַחַג   לְקַדְּשׁוֹ   הָעֶרֶב   הַמֶּלֶךְ

_____ _____ _____ _____ _____

_____ _____ _____ _____ _____

_____

.5 What does יְהוָה command us to do? Complete the missing words.

לְקַדְּשׁוֹ			אֶת־	זָכוֹר	שְׁמוֹת 20:8(7)
_ _ _	the Sabbath	day			Exodus 20:8(7)
					Normal English

6. Write in Hebrew: "Peaceful Sabbath".

_____   _____

7. What is the <u>root</u> meaning of אָ.מ.ן ?

_____

Write two Hebrew words that come from this root and their English meaning:

8. _____   _____

9. _____   _____

10. <u>If you have never celebrated שַׁבָּת</u>, I encourage you to begin! Below, explain why שַׁבָּת is important and ways you may like to celebrate this holy יוֹם. <u>If you are currently celebrating שַׁבָּת,</u> share some of your traditions below, and why they are meaningful to you.

<u>Use both English and Hebrew words to explain your answer:</u>

(Example: On עֶרֶב שַׁבָּת, my husband and I eat a special meal and say a בְּרָכָה over the bread and the wine.)

_____

_____

_____

_____

_____

_____

_____

4 - Passover פֶּסַח

חַג פֶּסַח שָׂמֵחַ!

A – Vocabulary

Memorize the following Hebrew words used in this lesson:

English	Gender	Transliteration	Hebrew	
bitter herbs	ms	ma-ROR	מָרוֹר	A1
leaven	ms	kha-METS	חָמֵץ	A2
life	ms	kha-YEEM	חַיִּים	A3
month	ms	KHO-desh	חֹדֶשׁ	A4
order (Passover service and meal)	ms	SE-der	סֵדֶר	A5
Passover	ms	PE-sakh	פֶּסַח	A6
sheaf (of grain)	ms	O-mer	עֹמֶר	A7
the telling (book used in the Passover service)	fs	ha-ga-DA	הַגָּדָה	A8
unleavened bread/s	fs, fpl	ma-TSA/ ma-TSOT	מַצָּה מַצּוֹת	A9

A11

The פֶּסַח Miracle

"Now when it happens that your children ask you, 'What does this ceremony mean to you?' You are to say, 'It is the sacrifice of ADONAI's פֶּסַח, because He passed over the houses of the Children of יִשְׂרָאֵל in Egypt, when He struck down the Egyptians, but spared our households.'" (Exodus 12:26-27)

When we celebrate the amazing story of פֶּסַח, we are honoring the command of יְהוָה to remember Israel's miraculous deliverance from Egyptian slavery into freedom through HIS mighty hand! The miracle that must be passed down to future generations!

"Because יְהוָה kept vigil that night to bring them out of Egypt, on this night all the Israelites are to keep vigil to honor יְהוָה for the generations to come." (Exodus 12:42)

B – Timing of פֶּסַח

B1

When are we to celebrate פֶּסַח?

"Observe the חֹדֶשׁ of Aviv and keep the פֶּסַח to יְהוָה your אֱלֹהִים, for in the חֹדֶשׁ of Aviv, יְהוָה your God brought you out from Egypt by night." (Deut. 16:1)

Although our Gregorian calendar begins on January 1st, GOD's holy calendar begins on the first יוֹם of the חֹדֶשׁ of אָבִיב (a-VEEV), meaning "spring," usually occurring in March or April. In Israel today, the month name is known as נִיסָן (nee-SAN) spelled "Nisan" in English, dating back to the Babylonian captivity.

To see a complete list of Biblical month names, see Appendix H.

Complete the missing words for Deut. 16:1 below.   **B2**

אֱלֹהֶיךָ	לַיהוָה		וְעָשִׂיתָ	הָאָבִיב		אֶת	שָׁמוֹר
your _____	____ ____	Passover	and* do	_____	month (of)	--	
							Normal English

*וּ (meaning "and") is a common prefix found in the Scriptures. In fact, if you look at an actual   **B3**
תּוֹרָה scroll, you will see that each column starts with a וּ!

C– Hebrew Root ח.ד.שׁ

Fill in the missing Hebrew word, then (circle) the root letters in the Hebrew words below.

Words from the Root		Root Meaning	Root
month			
months (kho-da-SHEEM)	חֳדָשִׁים		
new (ms)	חָדָשׁ	new, renew	ח.ד.שׁ used 286X In the Scriptures
new (fs) covenant (Jer. 31:30(31))	בְּרִית חֲדָשָׁה		
New Moon (head of the month) (Num. 10:10)	רֹאשׁ חֹדֶשׁ		

D- פֶּסַח Scriptures

Most people think of פֶּסַח as one holiday, but really it can be broken into   D1
three parts; פֶּסַח, Feast of Unleavened Bread and Waving of the עֹמֶר.
As you study each part, read and translate each Hebrew word <u>out loud</u>.

"This month will mark the beginning of months for you; it is to be the first month of the year for   D2
you. Tell the whole community of יִשְׂרָאֵל *that on the tenth day of this* חֹדֶשׁ *each man is to take*
a lamb for his family, one for each household. Take care of them until the fourteenth יוֹם *of the*
חֹדֶשׁ, *when all the members of the community of Israel must slaughter them at twilight. Then*
they are to take some of the blood and put it on the sides and tops of the doorframes of the
houses where they eat the lambs... They are to eat the meat that night, roasted over a fire.
With _____ *and* מָרוֹר *they are to eat it."* Exodus 12:2-3,6-8

unleavened breads

חַיִּים

By applying the sacrificial blood of the פֶּסַח lamb on the   D3
doorposts, the angel of death "passed over" the Hebrew
people, providing "חַיִּים" instead of death.

These doorposts were in the shape of the letter ח
(khet) which represents חַיִּים and חַי (khai) "live."
Hence, we have the beautiful tradition of Jewish women
wearing the חַי necklace to represent the incredible
importance of חַיִּים to the Jewish people.

E - The Feast of Unleavened Breads חַג הַמַּצּוֹת

"For seven יָמִים *you are to eat* מַצּוֹת, *but on the first* יוֹם *you must remove* חָמֵץ *from*   E1
your houses, for whoever eats חָמֵץ *from the first* יוֹם *until the*
seventh יוֹם, *that soul will be cut off from Israel."* Exodus 12:15

"And on the fifteenth יוֹם *of the same* חֹדֶשׁ *is the* חַג *of* הַמַּצּוֹת *to* יְהֹוָה; *for seven* יָמִים   E2
you shall eat מַצּוֹת. *On the first* יוֹם *you shall have a holy* מִקְרָא; *you shall not do any*
laborious מְלָאכָה. *But you shall present a food offering to the LORD for seven* יָמִים. *On the*
seventh _____ *is a holy* מִקְרָא; *you shall not do any laborious* מְלָאכָה." Leviticus 23:6-8

day

F. Waving the עֹמֶר

F1

"Speak to the Israelites and say to them: 'When you enter the land I am going to give you and you reap its harvest, bring to the priest an עֹמֶר of the first grain you harvest. He is to wave the עֹמֶר before יְהוָה so it will be accepted on your behalf; the priest is to wave it on the יוֹם after the שַׁבָּת.'" (Leviticus 23:10-11)

Counting the עֹמֶר

F2

"From the day after the שַׁבָּת, the day you brought the sheaf of the wave offering, count off seven full weeks." Leviticus 23:15

During פֶּסַח, we begin the "Counting of the עֹמֶר." This is not a tradition of men, but a command from יְהוָה! Each day, for seven weeks, we count the days. On the first day, we say "This is the <u>1st</u> day of the עֹמֶר." On day 2, "This is the <u>2nd</u> day of the עֹמֶר." The count continues for seven weeks.

Note: We'll learn more about the עֹמֶר as it leads us to the שָׁבוּעוֹת lesson.

G – Plurals

Most nouns and verbs in Hebrew have both a gender; "male" or "female" and a number; "singular" or "plural."   G1

The ◌ִים.. suffix (ending) indicates that a word is <u>masculine plural</u>. This suffix can also   G2
apply to mixed groups (both males and females). Example: יוֹם changes to יָמִים.

The ◌וֹת.. suffix shows that a word is <u>feminine plural</u>. Ex: בְּרָכָה changes to בְּרָכוֹת.   G3
Vowels and letters may change or drop in the plural form, and there are exceptions!

In the following plural words, (circle) the gender (M for masculine or F for feminine),   G4
<u>underline</u> the suffix, and write the English meaning below each word.

הַגָּדוֹת	חֳדָשִׁים	מַצּוֹת	יָמִים
M or F	M or F	M or F	M or F
_____	_____	_____	_____
_____		_____	

You can learn more about genders and plurals in *Biblical Hebrew with Joy!* Lesson 5.   G5

H – פֶּסַח Traditions

H1

Clean out the חָמֵץ

Due to the commandment to remove חָמֵץ from each home, many religious Jews bring in professional cleaners for the big job! Stores cover all products with _____ so they
<u>leaven</u>
cannot be sold during the פֶּסַח week. I remember visiting an Israeli hotel buffet a full week before the start of פֶּסַח and (sadly) they had already stopped serving their amazing bread!

סֵדֶר   H2

There are so many different ways of celebrating פֶּסַח. I grew up in a Jewish home where the סֵדֶר (the name for the פֶּסַח service and meal) was always held in our home with my Dad, Bob, leading us as a family. We always included friends who had never experienced a סֵדֶר. This tradition to eat the פֶּסַח meal inside a home comes from the first פֶּסַח in Egypt: Exodus 12:7: *"They are to take the blood and put it on the two doorposts and on the crossbeam of the <u>houses where they will eat it</u>."*

In recent years, many congregations have chosen to have community meals in large   H3
venues to share this beautiful מוֹעֵד with as many people as possible.

H4

ORDER!

The word סֵדֶר (meaning _____) comes from the root ס.ד.ר. which is the root of many words that are used today in Modern Hebrew. When asking how someone is doing, a typical response is בְּסֵדֶר (b-**SE**-der), loosely meaning "OK" but literally meaning "in order." Also, the name given to the Jewish prayer book, used during all of the מוֹעֲדִים is the סִדּוּר (see-DUR), which includes the "order" of each service.

הַגָּדָה   H5

The commandment to observe פֶּסַח dates back to Exodus 12:24, *"Obey these instructions as a lasting ordinance for you and your descendants."* However, in the thirteenth century, a special book, the הַגָּדָה was first designed to preserve these special prayers and traditions throughout the generations. הַגָּדָה means "telling," as it "tells" the story of פֶּסַח in a way that encourages participation by the whole family, especially the children. Today, there are thousands of הַגָּדוֹת worldwide which include different traditions, but all are an attempt to honor our Holy _____ by celebrating His מוֹעֵד.
GOD

Celebrating with friends in Tennessee

The beloved 1923 הַגָּדָה from my childhood

H6

I – Reading the Hallel

I1 Many of the Psalms are traditionally a part of the הַגָּדָה of פֶּסַח. Included are the הַלֵּל (ha-LEL "praise") Psalms 113 – 118 and Psalm 136, called the "Great" הַלֵּל (most likely used during Temple worship!) The "Great" הַלֵּל has a beautiful phrase that repeats over and over:

חַסְדּוֹ	לְעוֹלָם	כִּי
(is) His lovingkindness	to forever	for/because

I2 Read out loud the following Hebrew from Psalm 136:1. Circle words that you know.

הוֹדוּ לַיהוָה כִּי־טוֹב כִּי לְעוֹלָם חַסְדּוֹ:

"Give thanks to the LORD, for He is good. *His lovingkindness is forever!*

I3

Ancient הַלֵּל

The עִבְרִית root ה.ל.ל means "to shine" as we see in Job 29:2-3:

"... as in the days when God watched over me, when His lamp <u>shone</u> above my head, then by His light I walked through darkness... "

But ה.ל.ל can also mean "commend" or "praise." In ancient times, the North Star, unlike all other stars, remained motionless and constantly shone in the northern sky as a guide when traveling. So, in the Ancient עִבְרִית mind we "praise" יְהוָה by looking at Him as the guiding star that "shines" to show us our direction. הַלְלוּ־יָהּ!

adapted from *Ancient Hebrew Dictionary* by Jeff Benner

J – הַגָּדָה פֶּסַח

On the next six pages, you will find a "mini" version of a הַגָּדָה for פֶּסַח. It includes some of the Scriptures, prayers and traditions found in many of the הַגָּדוֹת. Please remember that this is only a guide, a starting point. Feel free to adjust it in any way. For a more complete הַגָּדָה, look for "Passover Haggadah" on the internet to find a huge number of choices!

Passover Haggadah

Happy Passover! khag PE-sakh sa-ME-akh! חַג פֶּסַח שָׂמֵחַ!

Leader: Why do we celebrate this holiday? Exodus 12:24-27 tells us to *"Obey these instructions as a <u>lasting ordinance</u> for you and your descendants. When you enter the land that the LORD will give you as he promised, observe this ceremony. And when your children ask you, 'What does this ceremony mean to you?' then tell them, 'It is the Passover sacrifice to the LORD, who passed over the houses of the Israelites in Egypt and spared our homes when he struck down the Egyptians.'"*

How do we tell the Passover story? We use a **"Hagadah"** הַגָּדָה meaning **"to tell"**; in this case, to tell the story of Passover, to tell of GOD's redemptive grace. The Hagadah was originally very brief but succeeding generations have added their interpretations and traditions. Today, there are thousands of versions of the Hagadah (including this one!).

What is a Passover **Seder**? **"SE-der"** סֵדֶר means **"order,"** therefore, the Hagadah presents the **order** of the Passover service.

The Four Cups of Wine

As we read through this Hagadah, we will drink from the cup of wine (or grape juice) four times. These four cups stand for four of the "I wills" recorded in Exodus 6:6-7:

The Cup of Sanctification "I will bring you out from under the burdens of the Egyptians"

The Cup of Judgment "I will rid you out of their bondage."

The Cup of Redemption "I will redeem you with an outstretched arm."

The Cup of Praise "I will take you to me for a people."

Kiddush קִדּוּשׁ - Blessing of the 1st Cup

The Cup of Sanctification
"I will bring you out from under the burdens of the Egyptians" (Exodus 6:6)
This is GOD's promise that He would bring the people out from the bondage of
Egyptian slavery.

Sing then drink together:

בָּרוּךְ אַתָּה יְהֹוָה אֱלֹהֵינוּ מֶלֶךְ הָעוֹלָם בּוֹרֵא פְּרִי הַגָּפֶן. אָמֵן.
*ba-ROOKH a-TA a-do-NAI, e-lo-**HAY**-noo **ME**-lekh ha-o-LAM, bo-RE p-REE ha-**GA**-fen. a-MEN*
Blessed are You, O LORD our GOD, King of the Universe, Who creates the fruit of the vine. Amen.

Khamets חָמֵץ "leaven"

Exodus 12:15 *For seven days you are to eat matsah מַצָּה (bread made without yeast). On the first day remove the "leaven" חָמֵץ from your houses, for whoever eats anything with leaven in it, from the first day through the seventh must be cut off from Israel.*

Typically, in the Bible, leaven is a symbol for sin, so to honor this commandment, before the beginning of Passover, we take all leaven (things with yeast that are puffy) out of our home.

HaMotsee הַמּוֹצִיא - Blessing Over the Matsah מַצָּה

Leader breaks the matsah into small pieces and distributes it to all.
Sing together:

בָּרוּךְ אַתָּה יהוה אֱלֹהֵינוּ מֶלֶךְ הָעוֹלָם הַמּוֹצִיא לֶחֶם מִן הָאָרֶץ. אָמֵן.

*ba-ROOKH a-TA a-do-NAI, e-lo-**HAY**-noo **ME**-lekh ha-o-LAM, ha-**MO**-tsee **LE**-khem meen ha-**A**-rets. a-MEN*
Blessed are You, O LORD our GOD, King of the Universe, Who brings forth bread from the earth.

(All eat a piece of matsah)

Blessing of the Ezov אֵזוֹב Hyssop

The greens (parsley) represent the hyssop which was used to place the blood of the Passover lamb upon the doorposts. The salt water represents the tears shed in Egypt and the Red Sea, both of which are salty.
Exodus 12:22 *"Take a **bunch of hyssop**, dip it into the blood in the basin and put some of the blood on the top and on both sides of the doorframe."*
The greens are dipped in salt water.

Leader reads, then all eat the greens:

בָּרוּךְ אַתָּה יְהוָה אֱלֹהֵינוּ מֶלֶךְ הָעוֹלָם בּוֹרֵא פְּרִי הָאֲדָמָה. אָמֵן.

*ba-ROOKH a-TA a-do-NAI, e-lo-**HAY**-noo **ME**-lekh ha-o-LAM, bo-RE p-REE ha-a-da-MAH. a-MEN*
Blessed are You, O LORD our GOD, King of the Universe, Who creates the fruit of the earth. Amen.

The Maggid הַמַגִּיד Retelling the Story of the Exodus

Exodus 12

³ *Speak to all the assembly of Israel and say, 'On the tenth day of this month, each man is to take a lamb or kid for his family, one per household.* ⁶ *'You are to keep it until the fourteenth day of the month, and then the entire assembly of the community of Israel will slaughter it at dusk.* ⁷ *They are to take some of the blood and smear it on the two sides and top of the doorframe at the entrance of the house in which they eat it.*

⁸ *That night, they are to eat the meat, roasted in the fire; they are to eat it with matsah (unleavened bread) and maror (bitter herbs).* ¹¹ *"'Here is how you are to eat it: with your belt fastened, your shoes on your feet and your staff in your hand; and you are to eat it hurriedly. It is ADONAI's [the LORD's] Pesach [Passover].*

¹² *For that night, I will pass through the land of Egypt and kill all the firstborn in the land of Egypt, both men and animals; and I will execute judgment against all the gods of Egypt; I am ADONAI.* ¹³ *The blood will serve you as a sign marking the houses where you are; when I see the blood, I will pass over you — when I strike the land of Egypt, the death blow will not strike you.*

¹⁴ *This will be a day for you to remember and celebrate as a festival to ADONAI; from generation to generation, you are to celebrate it by a perpetual regulation.* ¹⁵ *For seven days you are to eat matsah — on the first day remove the leaven from your houses. For whoever eats khamets [leaven or yeast] from the first to the seventh day is to be cut off from Israel.* ¹⁶ *On the first and seventh days, you are to have an assembly set aside for GOD. On these days no work is to be done, except what each must do to prepare his food; you may do only that."*

The Four Questions

Why is this night different from all other nights? *Asked by the youngest child:*

1. On all other nights, we eat either leavened bread or matsah. Why, on this night, do we eat only matsah?
2. On all other nights, we eat all kinds of herbs. Why, on this night, do we eat only bitter herbs?
3. On all other nights, we do not dip herbs. Why, on this night, do we dip them twice?
4. On all other nights, we eat sitting or reclining upon pillows. Why on this night, do we eat only reclining upon pillows?

The leader replies to the child:

I am glad you asked these questions! This night is different from all other nights because on this night we celebrate the going forth of the Hebrew people from slavery to freedom.

1. Why do we eat only matsah tonight?
As it is written in Exodus 12:8,39 *"The LORD commanded Moses to eat the meat roasted over the fire, along with bitter herbs and **bread made without yeast.** And they baked unleavened cakes of the dough which they had brought out of Egypt; for it was not leavened, because they were driven out of Egypt and could not wait, nor had they prepared provisions for themselves."*

2. Why do we eat bitter herbs tonight?
It is because the Egyptians made bitter the lives of our forefathers in Egypt, as it is written in Exodus 1:14: *"And they embittered their lives with harsh labor, with mortar and bricks and all sorts of work in the field, with all the tasks ruthlessly imposed upon them."* The bitter herbs speak of the sorrow, the persecution, and the suffering under the hand of Pharaoh; and as horseradish brings tears to the eyes, so, also, did the great affliction of the people bring tears to their eyes.

3. Why do we dip the herbs twice tonight? We dip the parsley in salt water to remind us of the tears of slavery. We dip the bitter herbs in sweet apples and honey to remind us that our forefathers withstood bitter slavery, sweetened by the hope of freedom.

4. Why do we recline at the table? Because reclining was a sign of a free man long ago, and since our forefathers were freed on this night, we recline at the table.

The Ten Plagues
Each person dips their finger in the wine/grape juice and puts a drop on their plate as the leader says each plague:
These are the 10 plagues, which the LORD brought on the Egyptians in Egypt.

Blood   Frogs   Gnats   Insects   Dead Livestock

Boils   Hail   Locusts   Darkness

Slaying of the First Born

Korban Pesakh קָרְבָּן פֶּסַח Passover Sacrifice
What does the lamb shank bone represent? It represents the miracle of Adonai sparing the houses of our ancestors in Egypt. This is the Passover sacrifice to the LORD who passed over the houses of the children of Israel when he struck Egypt and spared the Hebrew homes.
Exodus 12: 23: *"When the LORD goes through the land to strike down the Egyptians, he will see the blood on the top and sides of the doorframe and will pass over that doorway, and he will not permit the destroyer to enter your houses and strike you down."*

Kiddush קִדּוּשׁ   2nd Cup - The Cup of Judgment

Exodus 6:6 *"I will rid you out of their bondage."*

Sing together:

בָּרוּךְ אַתָּה יְהוָה אֱלֹהֵינוּ מֶלֶךְ הָעוֹלָם בּוֹרֵא פְּרִי הַגָּפֶן. אָמֵן.

ba-ROOKH a-TA a-do-NAI, e-lo-HAY-noo ME-lekh ha-o-LAM, bo-RE p-REE ha-GA-fen. a-MEN
Blessed are You, O LORD our GOD, King of the Universe, Who creates the fruit of the vine. Amen.
Drink the cup together.

Maror מָרוֹר   Bitter Herbs (traditionally horseradish)

Exodus 1:13-14 *"So the Egyptians made the children of Israel serve with rigor. And they made their lives bitter with hard bondage— in mortar, in brick, and in all manner of service in the field."*
All dip a piece of matsah into the bitter herbs. Leader reads:

ba-ROOKH a-TA a-do-NAI, e-lo-HAY-noo ME-lekh ha-o-LAM, v-tsee-VA-noo al a-kee-LOT ma-ROR.
Blessed are You, O LORD our GOD, King of the Universe, who commanded us to eat bitter herbs.
All eat the matsah and maror.

Kharoset חֲרוֹסֶת (mixture of chopped apples, spices, honey & wine/grape juice) is a symbol of

the mortar, representing the clay bricks which were made by the children of Israel in Egypt.
All take two pieces of matzah. Fill with kharoset (apples mixture) and the bitter herbs.
All eat the matsah sandwich together.

Passover Meal בְּתֵאָבוֹן b-te-a-VON! Bon Appetit!

The Kiddush קִדּוּשׁ 3rd Cup - The Cup of Redemption

This cup represents the third "I Will" from Exodus 6:6: *"I will redeem you."* This is GOD's promise that He would redeem his people, meaning He would buy them back.
Sing, and then drink the cup together:

בָּרוּךְ אַתָּה יְהוָה אֱלֹהֵינוּ מֶלֶךְ הָעוֹלָם בּוֹרֵא פְּרִי הַגָּפֶן. אָמֵן.

ba-ROOKH a-TA a-do-NAI, e-lo-HAY-noo ME-lekh ha-o-LAM, bo-RE p-REE ha-GA-fen. a-MEN
Blessed are You, O LORD our GOD, King of the Universe, Who creates the fruit of the vine. Amen.

Hallel – Praise – Psalm 136:1

הוֹדוּ לַיהוָה כִּי־טוֹב כִּי לְעוֹלָם חַסְדּוֹ:

Ho-DOO la-Adonai kee tov, kee l-o-LAM khas-DO

All – Give thanks to the LORD, for He is good, for his lovingkindness is forever!

The Kiddush קִדּוּשׁ   4th Cup - The Cup of Praise

(Exodus 6:7-8) "I will take you as my own people, and I will be your GOD . Then you will know that I am the LORD your GOD, who brought you out from under the yoke of the Egyptians. And I will bring you to the land I swore with uplifted hand to give to Abraham, to Isaac and to Jacob. I will give it to you as a possession. I am the LORD."

Sing, then drink together:

בָּרוּךְ אַתָּה יְהוָה אֱלֹהֵינוּ מֶלֶךְ הָעוֹלָם בּוֹרֵא פְּרִי הַגָּפֶן. אָמֵן.

*ba-ROOKH a-TA a-do-NAI, e-lo-**HAY**-noo **ME**-lekh ha-o-LAM, bo-RE p-REE ha-**GA**-fen. a-MEN*
Blessed are You, O LORD our GOD, King of the Universe, Who creates the fruit of the vine. Amen.

Final Prayer: **Leader: Now, our Passover is almost complete! Say boldly together:**

לְשָׁנָה הַבַּאָה בִּירוּשָׁלַיִם

l-sha-NA ha-ba-A bee-roo-sha-LAI-yeem!

Next Year in Jerusalem!

4 - Passover Exercises

שֵׁם _____

1. Read and be able to translate the following Hebrew words.

זָכוֹר מָרוֹר עֹנֶג חֹדֶשׁ סֵדֶר הַגָּדָה יוֹם קֹדֶשׁ חָמֵץ חַיִּים

שָׁמוֹר מַצָּה עֹמֶר לְקָדְשׁוֹ מוֹעֲדִים עֶרֶב פֶּסַח חֶסֶד

2. What is the English meaning of the following plural words?

מַצּוֹת   בְּרָכוֹת   הַגָּדוֹת   יָמִים   חֳדָשִׁים

_____   _____   _____   _____   _____

_____   _____

3. Fill in the missing words below for the "Great" Hallel from Psalm 136:1.

חַסְדּוֹ	לְעוֹלָם	כִּי	כִּי־טוֹב	לַיהוָה	הוֹדוּ
____	____		for good	____ ____	give thanks
					Normal English

4. Why do we celebrate Passover?

_____

_____

_____

5. What is the root meaning of ח.ד.שׁ ?

_____

Write two Hebrew words that come from this root and their English meaning.

6. _____   _____

7. _____   _____

Passover פֶּסַח Puzzle

Use the following עִבְרִית (Hebrew) words to complete the crossword puzzle:

פֶּסַח   מָרוֹר   חָמֵץ   מַצָּה   עֹמֶר   קִדּוּשׁ   הַגָּדָה   סֵדֶר

שׁ F	ו	ד	ק	1
			H A	2
			D	3
			G	4
		B		5
	E		C	6
				7
				8

Don't use vowels marks!

1. traditional blessing over the wine
2. leaven
3. order
4. bitter herbs
5. traditional book read during Passover
6. Passover (Passover offering)
7. sheaf
8. unleavened bread

9. What is the עִבְרִית greeting from the puzzle?

		שׁ						
H	G	F		E	D	C		B	A

10. Every year, as the סֵדֶר of פֶּסַח is finished, on the last page of the הַגָּדָה, these final words are spoken loudly in unison with expectant hope by all! <u>Draw syllable lines in the Hebrew words below</u>. Then, speak them out loud as a heart-felt prayer for the coming year!

לְשָׁנָה   הַבָּאָה   בִּירוּשָׁלַיִם!

to year   the coming   in Jerusalem

Next year in Jerusalem!

5 – Feast of Weeks שָׁבוּעוֹת

> חַג שָׁבוּעוֹת שָׂמֵחַ!

A – Vocabulary

Memorize the following Hebrew words used in this lesson.

English	Gender	Transliteration	Hebrew	
harvest	ms	ka-TSEER	קָצִיר	A1
first fruits	mpl	bee-koo-REEM	בִּכּוּרִים	A2
Ruth	fs	root	רוּת	A3
seven (fem)	fpl	**SHE**-va	שֶׁבַע	A4
seven (masc)	mpl	sheev-A	שִׁבְעָה	A5
week	ms	sha-**VOO**-a	שָׁבוּעַ	A6
weeks	mpl*	sha-voo-OT	שָׁבוּעוֹת	A7
you	ms	a-TA	אַתָּה	A8

* שָׁבוּעוֹת is a masculine word with a feminine plural ending – an exception!

B – שָׁבוּעוֹת Scriptures

During פֶּסַח, we begin the counting of the עֹמֶר which leads us to שָׁבוּעוֹת, also called **B1**
חַג הַקָּצִיר meaning _____.

Leviticus 23:15-17 *"From the יוֹם after the שַׁבָּת, the יוֹם you brought* **B2**
the עֹמֶר *of the wave offering, count off* שֶׁבַע *full* שַׁבָּתוֹת*. Count off fifty* יָמִים *up to the*
יוֹם *after the seventh* שַׁבָּת*, and then present an offering of new grain* לַיהוָה*. You are to*
bring out of your houses two loaves of bread for a wave offering, made of two tenths of an
ephah of fine flour. They are to be baked with חָמֵץ *as* _____ *to* יהוָה*."*
first fruits

Exodus 34:22 *"*אַתָּה *are to observe the Feast of* שָׁבוּעוֹת*, which is the* **B3**
קָצִיר בִּכּוּרִים *of the wheat."*

Numbers 28:26 *"On the* יוֹם *of* הַבִּכּוּרִים*, when* אַתָּה *offer* לַיהוָה *a new grain offering* **B4**
during שָׁבוּעוֹת *you are to have a holy* מִקְרָא*.* אַתָּה *shall not do any laborious* מְלָאכָה*."*

As we have read in the Scriptures, during פֶּסַח we celebrate the barley קָצִיר and during **B5**
שָׁבוּעוֹת we celebrate the בִּכּוּרִים of the wheat _____.
harvest

Book of רוּת

B6

At what time of year did the events of the Book of Ruth take place?
The answer is found in רוּת 2:23: "*So* רוּת *stayed close to the women of Boaz to glean until the* קָצִיר *of barley and the* קָצִיר *of wheat were finished.*"

As the story took place during the barley and wheat harvests, the beautiful tradition developed of reading the entire book of _____ during שָׁבוּעוֹת.

Ruth

C – Giving of the Torah מַתָּן הַתּוֹרָה

As we've learned from the שָׁבוּעוֹת Scriptures, this חַג is an agricultural מוֹעֵד honoring יהוה for the קָצִיר. As the children of יִשְׂרָאֵל left Egypt on the way to the Promised Land, it was impossible for them to harvest crops in the desert wilderness. But, 50 days after the first פֶּסַח in Egypt, an amazing event took place! **C1**

Exodus 19:1 "*On the first* יוֹם *of the third month after the Israelites left Egypt - on that very* יוֹם *- they came to the Desert of Sinai.*" Three יָמִים later, in Exodus 20:1-17, יהוה first speaks the words of the beloved Ten Commandments עֲשֶׂרֶת הַדְּבָרִים (a-**SE**-ret ha-d-va-REEM). **C2**

Ex. 29:43 "*I will meet with the sons of* יִשְׂרָאֵל *there. So it will be sanctified by My* כָּבוֹד." **C3**

Because of the timing of this "first" שָׁבוּעוֹת, 50 days after the first פֶּסַח, people worldwide celebrate this מוֹעֵד to thank יהוה for His holy "instruction book," the _____, and to recommit their lives to serving Him.

instruction

In the Wilderness

C4

Although the desert seems (on the surface) to be a place that is hostile to חַיִּים, the עִבְרִית language shows us that the spiritual wilderness experience can be an extremely valuable time of growing in our relationship with יהוה. The word "meed-BAR" (desert), מִדְבָּר contains the exact same letters as "m-da-BER" מְדַבֵּר which is the עִבְרִית word for "speak or talk." It is in the wilderness times of our lives that God can speak a "word in due season" to our hearts. Hannah Nesher www.voiceforisrael.net

And it was in this desert wilderness that יהוה spoke and wrote the living words of His instruction book – the תּוֹרָה!

D – Blessing the Giver of the תּוֹרָה

Through the centuries, the reading of the תּוֹרָה has become an integral part of   D1
Jewish synagogue worship. In order to thank יְהֹוָה for this precious gift, the
following traditional prayer is recited before the reading of the תּוֹרָה.

To hear the prayer, go to hebrewwithjoy.com/hjbf-audios/ and click on   D2
Torah Blessings. Then, practice reading, and circle the words that you know.

בָּרְכוּ אֶת יְהֹוָה הַמְּבֹרָךְ.

בָּרוּךְ יְהֹוָה הַמְּבֹרָךְ לְעוֹלָם וָעֶד.

בָּרוּךְ אַתָּה יְהֹוָה אֱלֹהֵינוּ מֶלֶךְ הָעוֹלָם,

אֲשֶׁר בָּחַר בָּנוּ מִכָּל הָעַמִּים

וְנָתַן לָנוּ אֶת תּוֹרָתוֹ:

בָּרוּךְ אַתָּה יְהֹוָה, נוֹתֵן הַתּוֹרָה. אָמֵן

Leader: Bless the LORD, the Blessed One.   D3
    All: Blessed is the LORD, the Blessed One, throughout all time.
Leader: Blessed are you, LORD our God, King of the universe,
    Who has chosen us from among all peoples
    And has given us His Instruction.
    All: Blessed are You, LORD, giver of the Instruction. Amen

Complete the last line of the prayer in the chart below.

אָמֵן	הַתּוֹרָה.	נוֹתֵן		אַתָּה		
	——	giver (of)	LORD		blessed (are)	D4

E – Hebrew Numbers

Unlike English, the עִבְרִית "cardinal" numbers (1, 2, 3) have both a masculine and feminine form and must match the gender of the words they describe. E1

E2

Masculine Numbers			*Feminine Numbers*		
e-KHAD	אֶחָד	1	*a-KHAT*	אַחַת	1
*sh-**NA**-yeem*	שְׁנַיִם	2	*sh-**TA**-yeem*	שְׁתַּיִם	2
sh-lo-SHA	שְׁלוֹשָׁה	3	*sha-LOSH*	שָׁלוֹשׁ	3
ar-ba-A	אַרְבָּעָה	4	*ar-BA*	אַרְבַּע	4
kha-mee-SHA	חֲמִשָּׁה	5	*kha-MESH*	חָמֵשׁ	5
shee-SHA	שִׁשָּׁה	6	*shesh*	שֵׁשׁ	6
sheev-A	שִׁבְעָה	7	***SHE**-va*	שֶׁבַע	7

*This section is an introduction to numbers only. You do not need to memorize all these examples. Refer to Appendix J1 to see more numbers.

Normally the number <u>precedes</u> the noun it describes. However, the number "one" always <u>follows</u> it! Fill in the following English translations. E3

Masculine Examples:

שִׁבְעָה חֳדָשִׁים
seven ___________

שְׁלוֹשָׁה יָמִים
three ___________

יְהוָה אֶחָד
___________ one

Feminine Examples:

שֶׁבַע שַׁבָּתוֹת
seven ___________

שָׁלוֹשׁ בְּרָכוֹת
three ___________

בְּרָכָה אַחַת
___________ one

Using the chart above for the following phrases, circle masculine or feminine, then translate into English. E4

קָצִיר אֶחָד	בְּרָכָה אַחַת	שֶׁבַע בְּרָכוֹת	אַרְבָּעָה יָמִים	שִׁשָּׁה חֳדָשִׁים	שְׁתַּיִם שַׁבָּתוֹת
M or F	M or F	M or F	M or F	M or F	M or F

If you are counting, the <u>feminine</u> form of the number is always used. For example, if you are taking a photo of a group, in English you would say, "one, two, three, …!"   E5

In עִבְרִית, you would say…

שָׁלוֹשׁ…	שְׁתַּיִם	אַחַת
3	2	1
sha-LOSH	sh-**TA**-yeem	a-KHAT

The Hebrew "ordinal" numbers (first, second, third) also have both a masculine and feminine form. Examples: seventh (m) = שְׁבִיעִי (sh-vee-EE) and seventh (f) = שְׁבִיעִית (sh-vee-EET). To see more ordinal number examples, refer to Appendix J2.   E6

E7

Holy Number שֶׁבַע

As we study the Holy words of יְהֹוָה, the number שֶׁבַע signifies perfection and completion. As we see in Genesis 2:2, *"By the seventh* יוֹם *God had finished the* מְלָאכָה *He had been doing; so on the seventh* יוֹם *He rested from all his* מְלָאכָה*."*

We also see the significance of שֶׁבַע as we count 7 weeks X 7 days = 49 days after the שַׁבָּת during פֶּסַח to celebrate שָׁבוּעוֹת on the 50th יוֹם.

F – Hebrew Root שׁ.ב.ע

Fill in the missing words, then (circle) the root letters in the Hebrew words below.

Words from the Root		Root Meaning	Root	
(f)	שֶׁבַע			F1
seven (m)	שִׁבְעָה			
seventh (m)	שְׁבִיעִי	seven	שׁ.ב.ע used 394X In the Scriptures	
week				
Have a good week!	שָׁבוּעַ טוֹב!			
	שָׁבוּעוֹת			
oath*	שְׁבוּעָה			

*In ancient times, an oath was promised once it was spoken out loud 7 times!   F2

G – Traditions of שָׁבוּעוֹת

Night Watch G1

*"My eyes are up before every **night watch**, as I meditate on Your word."*
(Psalm 119:148)

When the children of Israel were exiled from the Land, they could no longer celebrate שָׁבוּעוֹת as a קָצִיר festival. The ceremony was replaced with a sacred time to glorify and honor the giving of the תוֹרָה. Around the world, many communities celebrate by staying up all night for the "night watch," reading and studying a small portion of every book of the תוֹרָה!

Only In יִשְׂרָאֵל! G2

Those living in Jerusalem observe the "night watch" tradition by walking to the Western (Wailing) Wall הַמַּעֲרָבִי הַכּוֹתֶל (ha-ma-a-ra-VEE ha-ko-TEL). What a privilege to study תוֹרָה and pray with others at the site of the original Temple wall!

In the Kibbutseem and Moshaveem (communal settlements), spring harvest parties and parades are held complete with wagons and tractors. Homes are decorated with greenery and flowers and girls will often wear a זֵר פְּרָחִים (zer p-ra-KHEEM) "wreath of flowers" in their hair to honor the spring harvest.

Ten Commandments G3

During the שָׁבוּעוֹת service, the Ten Commandments are "canted" aloud (sung by a Cantor using the cantillation marks found in the Scriptures.) To hear these beautiful verses sung by Jennifer Casale, turn to the next page to access the QR code, and go to her YouTube channel (Hebrew Meadow).

שָׁבוּעוֹת Foods G4

As the priests were commanded in תוֹרָה to wave two loaves of bread to honor the gift of the קָצִיר, on שָׁבוּעוֹת, we eat two loaves of bread made with חָמֵץ.

It is also traditional to eat dairy products on שָׁבוּעוֹת, especially cheese blintzes and cheesecake, symbolizing that the תוֹרָה is as nutritional as "milk" and as sweet as "honey." Also, the תוֹרָה calls the land of יִשְׂרָאֵל a land "flowing with milk and honey." (Exodus 3:8) In Israel, שָׁבוּעוֹת is celebrated in the beautiful springtime with family picnics, enjoying the fruits of the land.

H - Personal שָׁבוּעוֹת Prayer

Write the missing Hebrew words on the lines below, then read it <u>out loud</u> to יְהוָה.

Dear _____, thank _____ for _____. You commanded us
            LORD   you   Feast of Weeks

to bring our _____ of the _____ to You. Thank _____
                    first fruits   harvest   you

for blessing us by giving us Your _____. Help us to obey your
                                         instruction

commands and give _____ honor every _____. _____
                     you   day   so be it

I –Celebrating שָׁבוּעוֹת

Below is a list of suggested activities that could be included in your
own personal שָׁבוּעוֹת celebration.

1. Read the following Scriptures:
    Exodus 19:1-20:23, 34:22, Leviticus 23:15-16, 21-22, Numbers 28:26

2. Read and listen to Jennifer Casale "cant" the Ten Commandments at
    youtu.be/jal48e1x2zM (or scan QR Code).

3. Read the entire book of רוּת.

4. If you have a group celebrating together, pick out a favorite short Psalm
    (like Psalm 117.)   Read it out loud in as many languages as possible.

5. Spend time in worship, praise, and prayer to יְהוָה, thanking Him for the
    קָצִיר season and for the giving of the תּוֹרָה.

6. Decorate your home with greenery and fresh flowers to remind you of the spring
    harvest and the command to bring your בִּיכּוּרִים to יְהוָה.

7. Go outside and enjoy a harvest picnic (or if it's too cold, create
    a festive meal indoors!). Don't forget the dairy products, especially the
    cheesecake! Include as many fruits and vegetables as possible in your meal.

8. Make your own flower crowns as a special springtime activity.
    (Use fresh flowers, craft wire and floral tape.)

שֵׁם _____   5 – Feast of Weeks Exercises

1. Read and be able to translate the following Hebrew words.

בִּיכּוּרִים קָצִיר שָׁבוּעַ עֹנֶג חֹדֶשׁ סֵדֶר מוֹעֲדִים יוֹם רוּת

לְקַדְּשׁוֹ שֶׁבַע שִׁבְעָה פֶּסַח עֹמֶר מִקְרָא שָׁמוֹר שָׁבוּעוֹת חַיִּים

2. Write the English meaning of each Hebrew phrase below. Refer to the chart in section E3.

שֵׁשׁ שַׁבָּתוֹת   אַרְבָּעָה שָׁבוּעוֹת   חָמֵשׁ בְּרָכוֹת

_____   _____   _____

תּוֹרָה אַחַת   קָצִיר אֶחָד   שְׁלוֹשָׁה חַגִּים

_____   _____   _____

3. Fill in the missing words below for the traditional תּוֹרָה blessing.

		נוֹתֵן			בָּרוּךְ
Amen	the instruction		LORD	you (ms)	_____ (are)

4. In your own English words, write the reasons for celebrating שָׁבוּעוֹת.

_____

_____

5. What is the root meaning of שׁ.ב.ע ?

_____

Write two Hebrew words that come from this root and their English meaning.

6. _____H   _____H
7. _____E   _____E

5 - Mid Quiz

At the beginning of this course, you took a Pre-Quiz to see how much of the course content you already knew. You are now half-way through the book! Now is the time to take the Mid-Quiz to see much you much you have learned. <u>Please DO NOT use any resources to complete this page</u>.

1. Match the words to their meaning.

first fruits	F	קָצִיר	A
guard/keep	____	שֶׁבַע	B
week	____	אַתָּה	C
harvest	____	שָׁבוּעוֹת	D
appointed time	____	פֶּסַח	E
Hebrew	____	בִּיכּוּרִים	F
month	____	בְּרָכָה	G
holy, holiness	____	יוֹם	H
sheaf of grain	____	שָׁמוֹר	I
weeks	____	קֹדֶשׁ	J
LORD	____	עֹמֶר	K
you (ms)	____	מוֹעֵד	L
blessing	____	חֶסֶד	M
Passover	____	שָׁבוּעַ	N
day	____	עִבְרִית	O
seven	____	יְהוָה	P
universe/world/forever	____	עוֹלָם	Q

2. Match the words to their meaning.

telling	____	חָמֵץ	A
Israel	____	עֹנֶג	B
sanctification	____	מָרוֹר	C
GOD	____	עֶרֶב	D
evening	____	זָכוֹר	E
life	____	מְלָאכָה	F
happy	____	סֵדֶר	G
blessed	____	חַיִּים	H
work	____	הַגָּדָה	I
bitter herbs	____	קִדּוּשׁ	J
holiday	____	שָׂמֵחַ	K
convocation	____	מוֹעֲדִים	L
order	____	מִקְרָא	M
appointed times	____	חַג	N
delight	____	אֱלֹהִים	O
remember	____	יִשְׂרָאֵל	P
leaven	____	בָּרוּךְ	Q

3. Match the roots to their meaning.

A. ח.ד.שׁ   B מ.ל.ך   C. שׁ.ב.ע   D. א.מ.ן

seven_____   truly_____   new, renew_____   rule, reign_____

Translate the עִבְרִית phrases into English.

	חַג שָׁבוּעוֹת שָׂמֵחַ .4
	בָּרוּךְ אַתָּה יְהוָה .5
	שַׁבָּת שָׁלוֹם .6

6 - Day of Blasting יוֹם תְּרוּעָה

חַג יוֹם תְּרוּעַה שָׂמֵחַ!
*To a good and sweet year!   לְשָׁנָה טוֹבָה וּמְתוּקָה!
*Traditional Rosh Hashana blessing for the new agricultural and civil year

A – Vocabulary

Memorize the following Hebrew words used in this lesson.

English	Gender	Transliteration	Hebrew	
blast/shout	fs	t-roo-A	תְּרוּעָה	A1
good (fem)	fs	to-VA	טוֹבָה	A2
good (masc)	ms	tov	טוֹב	A3
head	ms	rosh	רֹאשׁ	A4
remembrance	ms	zee-ka-RON	זִכָּרוֹן	A5
no, not	-	lo	לֹא	A6
ram's horn	ms	sho-FAR	שׁוֹפָר	A7
year	fs	sha-NA	שָׁנָה	A8

A10

I thought it was called "Rosh Hashana"

In September or October, Jews worldwide celebrate רֹאשׁ הַשָּׁנָה "Rosh Hashanah" as the beginning of their civil and agricultural calendar שָׁנָה, starting in the seventh Biblical חֹדֶשׁ. In Jewish חַיִּים, רֹאשׁ הַשָּׁנָה is also the start of the "High Holy Days," referring to the time between רֹאשׁ הַשָּׁנָה and the day of the Atonements.

As a child, my family attended רֹאשׁ הַשָּׁנָה services every שָׁנָה.
I remember these as somber times, with services lasting most of the day.
It was so different from our American New Year's celebration!

רֹאשׁ הַשָּׁנָה is not found in the Scriptures! Instead, the Biblical name of the מוֹעֵד is יוֹם תְּרוּעָה — the Day of Shouting or Blasting (of the trumpets). יוֹם תְּרוּעָה is celebrated as the first of the fall מוֹעֲדִים.

Scriptures יוֹם תְּרוּעָה – B

Another name for this מוֹעֵד is a "Day of the Memorial/Remembrance of Blasting." **B1**
יוֹם הַזִכָּרוֹן תְּרוּעָה (yom ha-zee-ka-RON t-roo-AH). Israeli Memorial Day, usually
celebrated in May, has a similar name: יוֹם הַזִכָּרוֹן.

Leviticus 23:24-25 *"Speak to the children of Israel, saying: 'In the seventh חֹדֶשׁ, on the* **B2**
first יוֹם of the חֹדֶשׁ, you shall have a שַׁבָּת rest, a זִכָּרוֹן of תְּרוּעָה (of the שׁוֹפָר),
a מִקְרָא-קֹדֶשׁ. You are לֹא to do laborious מְלָאכָה.'"

Numbers 29:1 *"On the first יוֹם of the seventh חֹדֶשׁ you are to have a מִקְרָא-קֹדֶשׁ. You* **B3**
are לֹא to do laborious מְלָאכָה. It is for you a יוֹם for תְּרוּעָה (of the שׁוֹפָר)."

From Numbers 29:1, what three commands does יְהוָה give us? Complete the chart.

לָכֶם	יְהְיֶה	קֹדֶשׁ	מִקְרָא-	בַּמִדְבָּר 29:1	B4
_____ you (mpl)	it shall be		_____ of	*Numbers 29:1	

* See Appendix K for a list of the Hebrew Books of the Tanakh (Old Testament)

תַעֲשׂוּ		עֲבֹדָה	מְלֶאכֶת	כָּל-	B5
you (mpl) will do	not	laborious		all	

לָכֶם	יְהְיֶה	תְּרוּעָה		B6
_____ you (mpl)	it shall be		day	

Sound of the שׁוֹפָר   **B7**

During יוֹם תְּרוּעָה we hear repeated blasts of the שׁוֹפָר. The root for שׁוֹפָר
is שׁ.פ.ר which means "to shape" or "to improve." The blasts are a
wake-up call to cause us to change, to be renewed, to draw us closer to our
Creator and to be changed into His image! When the שׁוֹפָר is blasted, we are
to seek יְהוָה with all our hearts and repent for the sin in our lives.

"Blow the שׁוֹפָר in Zion; sound the alarm on my holy hill. Let all who live in the
land tremble, for the יוֹם of יְהוָה is coming. It is close at hand." Joel 2:1

C – Hebrew Root ר.א.שׁ

Fill in the missing עִבְרִית word, then (circle) the root letters in the Hebrew words below.

Words from the Root		Root Meaning	Root
head		head, beginning	ר.א.שׁ used 598X In the Scriptures
head of the month (New Moon) Num. 10:10	רֹאשׁ חֹדֶשׁ		
first (ms)*	רִאשׁוֹן		
Sunday** (first day)	יוֹם רִאשׁוֹן		
first month	חֹדֶשׁ רִאשׁוֹן		

C1

*To see more ordinal numbers (first, second, third…) refer to Appendix J2   C2
**To see the Hebrew Days of the Week, refer to Appendix I.

D – Hebrew Months

In the Scriptures, most עִבְרִית months are named "first month, second month, third month…" D1
However, four of the חֳדָשִׁים are also given a different Biblical name. Two examples are on the
chart below. The first חֹדֶשׁ is also called "Aviv" (a-VEEV) and the seventh חֹדֶשׁ is called
"Etanim" (e-ta-NEEM). After the Babylonian captivity, the חֹדֶשׁ names were changed to
Babylonian names which are still used in יִשְׂרָאֵל today. For example, the first חֹדֶשׁ name was
changed to "Nisan" (nee-SAN) and the seventh month became "Tishrei" (teesh-RAY).

Time of Year	Number of Days	Post-exile English Transliteration	Post-exile Hebrew Name	Biblical English Name	Biblical Hebrew Name	Month #
Mar-Apr	30	Nisan	נִיסָן	Aviv (Exodus 13:4) 1st month	אָבִיב חֹדֶשׁ רִאשׁוֹן	1
Sept-Oct	30	Tishrei	תִּשְׁרֵי	Etanim (1 Kings 8:2) 7th month	אֵתָנִים חֹדֶשׁ שְׁבִיעִי	7

D2

Use the Hebrew Month Chart in Appendix H to complete the following.   D3
Just as the number שֶׁבַע indicates perfection and completion, the seventh חֹדֶשׁ is also

honored as קָדוֹשׁ. In preparation, during _____,
Biblical Hebrew name of 6th month (in Hebrew)
known today as "Elul," the שׁוֹפָר is sounded every יוֹם as a reminder to examine our
hearts prior to יוֹם תְּרוּעָה and to be ready to draw closer to יְהוָה during the "holy"
_____ חֹדֶשׁ of _____.
seventh (in Hebrew)   Post-exile name (in Hebrew)

E – Traditions of יוֹם תְּרוּעָה

Ten Days of Repentance   E1

Jewish people believe that on רֹאשׁ הַשָּׁנָה, our אֱלֹהִים opens His "Book of חַיִּים" to examine our deeds, and ten יָמִים later, on יוֹם הַכִּפֻּרִים, the book is closed. This period between the מוֹעֲדִים is called the "Ten Days of Repentance" עֲשָׂרָה יְמֵי תְּשׁוּבָה יָמִים נוֹרָאִים (a-sa-RA ya-MAY t-shoo-VA), the "Days of Awe" (ya-MEEM no-ra-EEM) or literally the "Terrible Days." This time is an opportunity to ask יְהֹוָה to forgive our personal sins and seek reconciliation from anyone we may have offended during the שָׁנָה. Daniel 12:1 *"But at that time your people—everyone who is found written in the book—will be delivered."*

Two יוֹם Celebration   E2

According to Jewish tradition, רֹאשׁ הַשָּׁנָה is regularly celebrated over two days because of the uncertainty of predicting which day the new moon will be sighted—signaling the start of the new חֹדֶשׁ.

Synagogue Services   E3

In Judaism, it is traditional to spend most of the day at the synagogue where the _____ is blown 100 times in unique combinations (long and short blasts).
ram's horn
The story of the binding of Isaac is read from Genesis 22, called עֲקֵידָה (a-kay-DA) or "binding" in עִבְרִית. This story shows the miraculous power of יְהֹוָה to supply what we need if we are faithful to obey His voice. He is our מֶלֶךְ!

"You will throw" tash-leekh תַּשְׁלִיךְ   E4

As we prepare for יוֹם הַכִּפֻּרִים, we זְכוֹר the people whom we have offended and the sins that we are still carrying. During רֹאשׁ הַשָּׁנָה, it is traditional to throw stones or pieces of bread (each representing a sin in our lives) into a running body of water. As we seek the forgiveness of יְהֹוָה, we can know in our hearts that He will carry our sins away "...as far as the east is from the west." *"You will subdue our iniquities, and you will throw all our sins into the depths of the sea."* Micah 7:19

רֹאשׁ הַשָּׁנָה Traditional Foods   E5

Apples dipped in honey represent the sweetness of a new שָׁנָה. A sweet round braided challah bread (which looks like a crown) is eaten to symbolize the kingship of יְהֹוָה and the circle of חַיִּים. Because רֹאשׁ הַשָּׁנָה means "head of the שָׁנָה," it is customary to eat the head of a fish דָּג (dag!) as we remember the promise from Deuteronomy 28:13: *"*יְהֹוָה *will make* אַתָּה *the _____ , not the tail."*
head

F – Celebrating יוֹם תְּרוּעָה

F1   This section outlines Biblical יוֹם תְּרוּעָה suggestions based on the three commands from these Scriptures.

F2   Leviticus 23:24-25: *"Speak to the children of* יִשְׂרָאֵל, *saying: 'In the seventh* חֹדֶשׁ, *on the first* יוֹם *of the* חֹדֶשׁ, *you shall have a* שַׁבָּת*-rest, a* זִכָּרוֹן *of* תְּרוּעָה (of the שׁוֹפָר), *a* מִקְרָא־קֹדֶשׁ. *You are* לֹא *to do laborious* מְלָאכָה.'"

F3   Numbers 29:1: *"On the first* יוֹם *of the seventh* חֹדֶשׁ *you are to have a* מִקְרָא־קֹדֶשׁ. *You are* לֹא *to do laborious* מְלָאכָה. *It is for you a* יוֹם *for* תְּרוּעָה (of the שׁוֹפָר)."

Holy Convocation מִקְרָא־קֹדֶשׁ

F4   Gather a group together or meet as a congregation to celebrate on the first יוֹם of the seventh Biblical חֹדֶשׁ. Use this "מִקְרָא־קֹדֶשׁ" time to meet with יְהוָה.

Rest on שַׁבָּת

F5   Make this day a holy יוֹם, set apart from the ordinary! We are commanded לֹא to do business _____ and take a rest from the daily distractions of life.

        work

The תְּרוּעָה of the שׁוֹפָר!

F6   Plan a time of praise and worship and include the תְּרוּעָה of the שׁוֹפָר in your worship time. Ask each person to bring their שׁוֹפָר to your gathering. This is a time to "זָכוֹר" the miracles of יְהוָה. Ask each person to share how יְהוָה has intervened in a miraculous way.

F7   Read Scriptures which include the תְּרוּעָה of the שׁוֹפָר, to remember that the תְּרוּעָה of the שׁוֹפָר represents the voice of יְהוָה to His people.

Exodus 19:17-19 Psalm 98:4-6 Isaiah 18:3 Isaiah 27:12-13
Jeremiah 4:19 Ezekiel 33:2-5 Amos 3:6-7 Zephaniah 1:14-17

F8

> My favorite יוֹם תְּרוּעָה memory has been from "on high!"
> A few years ago, in Colorado Springs, a dear friend and amazing man of אֱלֹהִים, TC Kim, invited us to a community gathering in Palmer Park, overlooking the city. We danced, prayed over the city and then blew our שׁוֹפָרוֹת together. Sadly, the next year, after battling cancer, TC went to be with יְהוָה. We miss him greatly.

May the Sound of the שׁוֹפָר...

F9

May the sound of the שׁוֹפָר shatter our complacency and make us conscious of the corruptions in our lives.

May the sound of the שׁוֹפָר penetrate our souls and cause us to turn back to our Father in Heaven.

May the sound of the שׁוֹפָר break the bonds of the evil impulse within us and enable us to serve the Lord with a whole heart.

May the sound of the שׁוֹפָר renew our loyalty to the one true King and strengthen our determination to defy the false gods.

May the sound of the שׁוֹפָר awaken us to the enormity of our sins and the vastness of God's חֶסֶד for those who truly repent.

May the sound of the שׁוֹפָר summon us to service and stir us to respond, as did Abraham, "Here am I."

May the sound of the שׁוֹפָר recall the moment when we stood at Mount Sinai and uttered the promise: "All that the LORD has spoken, we will keep and obey."

May the sound of the שׁוֹפָר recall the promise of the ingathering of the exiles and stir within us renewed devotion to the Land of Israel.

May the sound of the שׁוֹפָר recall the vision of the prophets, of the day when Egypt, Syria, and Israel will live in peace.

May the sound of the שׁוֹפָר awaken us to the flight of time and summon us to spend our days with purpose.

May the sound of the שׁוֹפָר become our jubilant shout of joy on the day of the promised, long-awaited redemption.

May the sound of the שׁוֹפָר remind us that it is time to "proclaim liberty throughout the land to all the inhabitants thereof."

May the sound of the שׁוֹפָר enter our hearts; for blessed is the people that hearkens to its call.

(Author anonymous – from Hannah Nesher, VoiceforIsrael.net)

"Blessed is the nation that knows תְּרוּעָה."   Psalm 89:15(16)

6 – Day of Blasting Exercises   שֵׁם _____

1. Read and be able to translate the following Hebrew words.

שָׁבוּעַ עֹנֶג חֹדֶשׁ שָׁנָה טוֹבָה שׁוֹפָר זִכָּרוֹן מְלָאכָה תְּרוּעָה
לֹא רֹאשׁ שֶׁבַע שִׁבְעָה פֶּסַח מִקְרָא טוֹב שָׁבוּעוֹת קֹדֶשׁ

2. Write the Biblical English Name of each Hebrew month below. See Appendix H.

חֹדֶשׁ חֲמִישִׁי
_____

חֹדֶשׁ שְׁמִינִי
_____

חֹדֶשׁ שֵׁנִי
2nd month
_____

חֹדֶשׁ שְׁבִיעִי
_____

חֹדֶשׁ רִאשׁוֹן
_____

חֹדֶשׁ עֲשִׂירִי
_____

3. Fill in the missing Hebrew words from Leviticus 23:24-25.

"Speak to the children of יִשְׂרָאֵל, saying: "In the seventh _____ ,
month

on the first _____ of the חֹדֶשׁ, you shall have a _____ rest, a memorial of
day   Sabbath

_____ the _____ , a holy _____ .
blowing   ram's horn   convocation

You are _____ to do laborious _____ ."
not   work

4. In English, write three Biblical commandments for יוֹם תְּרוּעָה.

a. _____
b. _____
c. _____

5. Write the English meanings for the following Hebrew roots.

שׁ.ב.ת   ר.א.שׁ   ח.ד.שׁ
_____   _____   _____

מ.ל.ך   א.מ.ן   שׁ.ב.ע
_____   _____   _____

Find the יוֹם תְּרוּעָה Words   6.

In this puzzle, (circle) the Hebrew letters for the words numbered below.
(They may be horizontal, vertical or diagonal.)
Note that if the answer is two words, there are no spaces between the words

1. blast/shout   2. ram's horn   3. head   4. year   5. no, not
6. good   7. work   8. head of the year   9. day of blasting   10. month
11. appointed times   12. convocation   13. holiday   14. day

ה	ה	כ	א	ל	מ	נ	ל	ח	א	ז	ט	ף
ל	ל	כ	נ	ץ	כ	שׁ	ג	שׁ	ד	ב	ב	ק
ק	ז	א	ר	ק	מ	שׁ	ר	שׁ	ס	שׁ	ר	ץ
ה	ר	ו	ת	ת	ח	מ	ב	ו	ט	כ	י	ג
ט	מ	ל	ר	ו	ק	ז	י	פ	ץ	י	מ	ו
ו	ל	ו	ס	א	ה	ע	ו	ר	ת	ס	ו	י
ב	ע	א	ץ	ל	שׁ	פ	ס	כ	ת	ק	ע	ד
ה	כ	ב	ה	נ	שׁ	ה	שׁ	א	ר	ב	ד	ו
ל	ה	ת	ה	שׁ	ע	ת	א	שׁ	א	צ	י	שׁ
ו	מ	ת	ד	י	ל	שׁ	ת	ר	שׁ	כ	ס	מ

7 - Day of the Atonements יוֹם הַכִּפֻּרִים

> (May you) finish inscribed for good (in the book of חַיִּים).
>
> גְּמַר חֲתִימָה טוֹבָה.
>
> (g-MAR kha-tee-MA to-VA)

A – Vocabulary

Memorize the following Hebrew words used in this lesson.

English	Gender	Transliteration	Hebrew	
afflict, deny	ms	a-NA	עָנָה	A1
atone, atonement	ms	kee-POOR	כִּפֶּר	A2
clean, purified	ms	ta-HOR	טָהוֹר	A3
fast (abstain from something)	ms	tsom	צוֹם	A4
fire	fs	esh	אֵשׁ	A5
repentance	fs	t-shoo-VA	תְּשׁוּבָה	A6
sin	ms	khet	חֵטְא	A7
soul	fs	**NE**-fesh	נֶפֶשׁ	A8
your (mpl) GOD	ms	e-lo-hay-KHEM	אֱלֹהֵיכֶם	A9

A10   In most Jewish communities, the Biblical name of יוֹם הַכִּפֻּרִים "Day of the Atonements" has been shortened to יוֹם כִּפֻּר "Day of Atonement."

A11

The Most יוֹם קָדוֹשׁ

Ten days after יוֹם תְּרוּעָה we come to what is traditionally the most קָדוֹשׁ of יָמִים on the Jewish calendar, יוֹם הַכִּפֻּרִים. It is considered the "שַׁבַּת of שַׁבָּתוֹת" and is the יוֹם, during Temple times, that the High Priest entered the Holy of Holies and applied blood to the כַּפֹּרֶת, (ka-**PO**-ret) the atonement (mercy seat) "cover." After the Temple was destroyed, ending the sacrificial offerings to atone for חֵטְא, כִּפֶּר was achieved through personal acts of תְּשׁוּבָה.

יוֹם הַכִּפֻּרִים *is marked by a seeking of GOD's forgiveness and a realization that only by His great mercy do we continue to exist and enjoy His gift of* חַיִּים … *We must return to Him with full hearts, seek His forgiveness with* תְּשׁוּבָה *and determine to walk in His statutes.*
Tim Hegg, "Yom Kippur" from TorahResources.com

Scriptures יוֹם הַכִּפֻּרִים – B

B1 Leviticus 16:29-31 *"It is to be a statute to you forever, that in the seventh חֹדֶשׁ, on the tenth יוֹם of the חֹדֶשׁ, you are to עָנָה your souls, and are לֹא to do any kind of מְלָאכָה —both the native-born and the foreigner dwelling among you. For on this יוֹם, כִּפֶּר will be made for you, to טָהוֹר you. From all your sins you will be before יְהֹוָה. It is a שַׁבָּת of solemn rest to you, and you are to עָנָה your souls. It is a statute forever."*

B2 Leviticus 23:26-28 *"יְהֹוָה spoke to Moses, saying: 'However, the tenth יוֹם of this seventh חֹדֶשׁ is יוֹם הַכִּפֻּרִים, a מִקְרָא־קֹדֶשׁ to you, so you are to עָנָה yourselves. You are to bring an offering made by אֵשׁ to יְהֹוָה. You are לֹא to do any kind of מְלָאכָה on that set day, for it is יוֹם הַכִּפֻּרִים, to make כִּפֶּר for you before יְהֹוָה your God.'"*

B3 Practice reading Leviticus 23:26-27a below <u>out loud</u>. Use syllable lines and cantillation marks to help you pronounce the accented syllables correctly.

וַיְדַבֵּר יְהֹוָה אֶל־מֹשֶׁה לֵּאמֹר:

to say	Moses	to	LORD	and spoke

אַ֤ךְ בֶּעָשׂוֹר לַחֹדֶשׁ הַשְּׁבִיעִי הַזֶּה יוֹם הַכִּפֻּרִים

the atonements	day	this	the seventh	of month	in the tenth	surely

הוּא מִקְרָא ־ קֹדֶשׁ יִהְיֶה לָכֶם

for you	will be	holy	convocation	it (is)

Suffix כֶם – C

C1 <u>To WHOM</u> were these מוֹעֵד instructions written? Look at the last word above.

לְ + כֶם = לָכֶם

for/to	you (mpl)	for/to you (mpl)

C2 Read Leviticus 16:29. Which two groups made up the "you" that יְהֹוָה was writing to?

_____   _____

C3 In English, it is not always clear whether the words "you" and "your" refer to an individual or to a group. However, עִבְרִית has various suffixes (endings) which specify person, number, and gender. The כֶם suffix specifically signifies a group (plural you/your), whether only men or a mix of men and women. Vowels and/or letters may be added, changed, or dropped when adding a suffix.

C4 Write the English meaning of the words below. Remember to use "you" or "your."

אֱלֹהֵיכֶם _____   נַפְשֹׁתֵיכֶם _____

C5 You can learn more about suffixes in *Biblical Hebrew with Joy!* Lessons 5, 8 & 9.

D – The צוֹם that Pleases יְהוָה

Scripture clearly shows the penalty for those who dare to work or disobey the command to "עָנָה your _____" on this מוֹעֵד: They will be cut off and destroyed!   D1
_{soul}

Leviticus 23:29-30 *"For anyone who does not עָנָה himself on that יוֹם must be cut off from his people. Anyone who does any kind of _____ on that יוֹם,*   D2
_{work}
that person, I will destroy from among his people."

What does it mean to עָנָה yourself? Although Scripture does not give specific instructions in Leviticus, the traditional _____ is to abstain from all food and drink   D3
_{fast}
and from activities of pleasure (including marital relations).

Isaiah 58:6-7 describes a different kind of צוֹם, a צוֹם from unrighteousness: D4

"Is not this the צוֹם I choose: to release the bonds of wickedness, to untie the cords of the yoke, to let the oppressed go free, and to tear off every yoke? Is it לֹא to share your bread with the hungry, to bring the homeless poor into your house? When אַתָּה see the naked, to cover him, and not hide yourself from your own flesh and blood?"

E – Hebrew Roots כ.פ.ר and שׁ.ו.ב

Fill in the missing words, then circle the root letters in the Hebrew words below.

Words from the Root		Root Meaning	Root	
atonement		cover, protect	כ.פ.ר used 102X In the Scriptures	E1
	יוֹם הַכִּפֻּרִים			
atonement cover (mercy seat) Ex 25:20	כַּפֹּרֶת			
dome (skullcap)	כִּיפָּה			

Words from the Root		Root Meaning	Root	
repentance*		to return, turn back	שׁ.ו.ב used 1066X In the Scriptures	E2
turn, return, again	שׁוּב			
to return	לָשׁוּב			

*True תְּשׁוּבָה is not only feeling regret for past wrongs but is a conscious commitment to turn away from חֵטְא and return to יְהוָה.   E3

> **Yom Kippur War**   E4
>
> On October 6, 1973, an Arab coalition led by Egypt and Syria took advantage of the quietness and holiness of יוֹם הַכִּפֻּרִים by launching a surprise attack against יִשְׂרָאֵל. This "Yom Kippur" war lasted 19 days with a resounding victory for יִשְׂרָאֵל. Once again, יְהֹוָה protected the land and people that He loves.

F – Traditions of יוֹם הַכִּפֻּרִים

Ending the Ten יָמִים of תְּשׁוּבָה   F1

Jewish people believe that on יוֹם הַכִּפֻּרִים, GOD closes His "Book of חַיִּים" after examining our deeds for the prior ten-day period (also called the "יָמִים of Awe"). This time leading up to יוֹם הַכִּפֻּרִים is a time of תְּשׁוּבָה, to ask יְהֹוָה to forgive our personal חֵטְא and seek reconciliation from those we may have offended during the שָׁנָה.

Daniel 12:1 *But at that time your people—everyone who is found written in the book—will be delivered.*

Fasting צוֹם   F2

The traditional צוֹם (mentioned earlier) lasts for twenty-four hours (from sundown to sundown). In addition, it is customary to refrain from bathing, wearing oils or lotions, wearing jewelry, make up, or leather shoes (because of their comfort!). In יִשְׂרָאֵל, you will see people dressed up in their finest clothing yet wearing canvas tennis shoes!

Memorial Candle   F3

Many families burn a "Yahrzeit" (anniversary) candle throughout יוֹם הַכִּפֻּרִים to honor their deceased relatives and their names are spoken out loud during the service.

Wearing White   F4

White is worn by most people as a symbol of being טָהוֹר. Many Orthodox men wear a "kittel" (**KI**-tuhl) – a long white robe. Even the תּוֹרָה is covered with a white cloth!

> F5
>
> In 2004, I had the privilege of attending my first יוֹם הַכִּפֻּרִים service in יִשְׂרָאֵל. I was visiting my sister Pam (who lives in the Jerusalem suburb of Meveseret Zion) and I had brought a new dress with me for attending the synagogue service. As we walked out the door, a blanket of white greeted us as every person walking towards the synagogue was wearing white. My dress, however, was a beautiful shade of Israeli blue!

Synagogue Worship   F6

In Jewish synagogues worldwide, יוֹם הַכִּפֻּרִים is considered the holiest of all יָמִים and is the יוֹם of greatest attendance. In Orthodox synagogues, there are five different services (instead of the usual four) which focus on self-examination, deep introspection, forgiveness of חֵטְא and heartfelt תְּשׁוּבָה.

כָּל נִדְרֵי   All Vows   F7

Before sunset on יוֹם הַכִּפֻּרִים, the כָּל נִדְרֵי (kol need-RAY) prayer is chanted by the Cantor (music leader). The name, meaning "All Vows," is a request to be released from any pledges or vows made before יְהֹוָה that may have been broken during the שָׁנָה. This comes from the time in history when Jewish people were required to take an oath to change to another religion or be executed!

Wearing white to a   F8
יוֹם הַכִּפֻּרִים gathering

Only in יִשְׂרָאֵל   F9

For 24 hours in יִשְׂרָאֵל, on יוֹם הַכִּפֻּרִים, the driving stops (except for emergency vehicles). The roads are filled with walking pedestrians who need to be careful while the children have free reign on the roads! אַתָּה will see darting bicycles and skateboards, even on the main highways!

Breaking the _____   F10
fast

At the end of the יוֹם of solemn תְּשׁוּבָה, each family breaks the צוֹם with a light meal. This becomes a time of celebration and rejoicing as hearts are turned to the next מוֹעֵד, the Feast of Booths, סֻכּוֹת. The next יוֹם traditionally begins the building of the temporary dwelling called a סֻכָּה.

G – How to Honor יוֹם הַכִּפֻּרִים

> ## Coming Clean   G1
> The purpose of יוֹם הַכִּפֻּרִים is to "come clean" before יְהוָֹה.
> *"Atonement means the removal of the spiritual pollution left behind by ritual impurity, חֵטְא or transgression."* First Fruits of Zion, *The Festivals*
>
> *During this season,* יוֹם הַכִּפֻּרִים *has been the time that* יְהוָֹה *has prompted me to search my heart to see if I have offended anyone without asking for their forgiveness. What a joy that some very important relationships in my* חַיִּים *have been renewed and restored during this holy* מוֹעֵד.

Afflict/Deny עָנָה   G2

Throughout this lesson, we have talked about many traditional ways to עָנָה yourselves. However, because Scripture does not give specific instructions, *ask* יְהוָֹה *to show* אַתָּה what to do to honor His _____ on this special יוֹם.
                                   instruction

Holy Convocation מִקְרָא־קֹדֶשׁ   G3

This is the most holy day, set apart from the ordinary! We are commanded לֹא to do any kind of מְלָאכָה and focus solely on the sovereignty of יְהוָֹה. Meet as a congregation, small group or family to celebrate on the tenth יוֹם of the seventh Biblical חֹדֶשׁ. Use this "מִקְרָא־קֹדֶשׁ" time to worship, pray together, and meet with our awesome _____.
                                                                LORD

Offering by אֵשׁ G4

Even though we can no longer make Temple sacrifices by אֵשׁ to יְהוָֹה, we surely can make sacrifices of our time, resources, and gifts to bless others. We should continually be offering a "sacrifice of praise" to our Father, the מֶלֶךְ! Psalm 50:23 *"A sacrifice of praise honors Me, and to the one who orders his way, I will show the salvation of* אֱלֹהִים."

7 – Day of Atonements Exercises   שֵׁם _____

Read and be able to translate the following Hebrew words.   1.

תְּשׁוּבָה תְּרוּעָה חֵטְא חַיִּים חֹדֶשׁ צוֹם שָׁנָה עָנָה כִּפֶּר
מִקְרָא לֹא נֶפֶשׁ שֶׁבַע טָהוֹר שָׁבוּעוֹת אֵשׁ יִשְׂרָאֵל

From Leviticus 23:27, complete the chart.

	הַשְּׁבִיעִי	לַחֹדֶשׁ	בֶּעָשׂוֹר	אַךְ	וַיִּקְרָא 23:27	
2.	———— ————	of (the) ————	on the tenth	surely	———— 23:27	

	-	הוּא	הַכִּפֻּרִים		הַזֶּה	
3.	convocation (of)	it (is)	———— ————	day	this	

	אֶת־	וְעִנִּיתֶם	לָכֶם	יִהְיֶה	קֹדֶשׁ	
4.		———— you shall ————	————	will be		

	לַיהוָה	אִשֶּׁה	וְהִקְרַבְתֶּם	נַפְשֹׁתֵיכֶם	
5.	——— ——— ———	an offering made by ————	———— offer	————	

In English, write three Biblical commandments for יוֹם הַכִּפֻּרִים.   6.

a. _____

b. _____

c. _____

.7   What are the <u>root</u> meanings of כ.פ.ר ?

_____

.8   Write two Hebrew words that come from this root and their English meaning.

_____H   _____H

_____E   _____E

.9   What is the meaning of the Hebrew suffix "כֶם"? _____

In the following Scriptures from Leviticus 16:29-31, (circle) the "כֶם" suffixes then <u>underline</u> the roots you know. Finally, read one or more lines out loud.

29 וְהָיְתָה לָכֶם לְחֻקַּת עוֹלָם בַּחֹדֶשׁ הַשְּׁבִיעִי בֶּעָשׂוֹר
לַחֹדֶשׁ תְּעַנּוּ אֶת־נַפְשֹׁתֵיכֶם וְכָל־מְלָאכָה לֹא תַעֲשׂוּ
הָאֶזְרָח וְהַגֵּר הַגָּר בְּתוֹכְכֶם:

30 כִּי־בַיּוֹם הַזֶּה יְכַפֵּר עֲלֵיכֶם לְטַהֵר אֶתְכֶם מִכֹּל
חַטֹּאתֵיכֶם לִפְנֵי יְהוָה תִּטְהָרוּ:

31 שַׁבַּת שַׁבָּתוֹן הִיא לָכֶם וְעִנִּיתֶם אֶת־נַפְשֹׁתֵיכֶם חֻקַּת
עוֹלָם:

.10   Write the missing Hebrew words in the prayer below, then read it <u>out loud</u> to יְהוָה.

Dear _____, thanks for giving us _____ _____.
        LORD   the Atonements   day

Help us to know how to _____ ourselves on this most holy _____.
                                          deny/afflict   day

Give us your direction on how to _____. Help us to take a _____ rest and
                                                        fast   Sabbath

keep us from doing any laborious _____. Help us to be _____.
                                                    work   clean/pure

before You, mighty _____.   _____
                                GOD   so be it

8 - Feast of Booths סֻכּוֹת

Season/Time of our Joy   זְמַן שִׂמְחָתֵנוּ   (z-MAN seem-kha-**TE**-noo)

חַג סֻכּוֹת שָׂמֵחַ!

A – Vocabulary

Memorize the following Hebrew words used in this lesson.

English	Gender	Transliteration	Hebrew	
booth, tabernacle	fs	soo-KA	סֻכָּה	A1
booths, tabernacles	fpl	soo-KOT	סֻכּוֹת	A2
citron (large yellow fruit similar to a lemon)	ms	et-ROG	אֶתְרוֹג	A3
date palm branch (collection of palms, willow & leafy branches)	ms	loo-LAV	לוּלָב	A4
fruit	ms	p-REE	פְּרִי	A5
joy (noun)	fs	seem-KHA	שִׂמְחָה	A6
joy of...	fs	seem-KHAT	שִׂמְחַת	A7
sons/children of...	mpl	b-NAY	בְּנֵי	A8

A9

Why Celebrate סֻכּוֹת?

The Feast of סֻכּוֹת (shortened from חַג הַסֻּכּוֹת) is celebrated on the 15th day of Tishrei (7th month) and completes the Biblical cycle of the מוֹעֲדִים. It is a remembrance of the 40-year trek through the wilderness to the Promised Land and is an agricultural חַג celebrating the end of the קָצִיר season. סֻכּוֹת is sometimes called "The Feast" - the biggest חַג of the מוֹעֲדִים, a joyous celebration following the somber time of יוֹם הַכִּפֻּרִים and יוֹם תְּרוּעָה. During the existence of the Jerusalem Temple, סֻכּוֹת was the last of the three annual pilgrimage מוֹעֲדִים.

The Feast of סֻכּוֹת is sometimes called by other names. In the following sections, we will study the Scriptures and traditions associated with each name.

B — Feast of the Booths חַג הַסֻּכּוֹת

Leviticus 23:34, 41-43   "³⁴*Speak to* בְּנֵי יִשְׂרָאֵל*, and say, 'on the fifteenth* יוֹם *of this seventh* חֹדֶשׁ *is* _____ *for seven* יָמִים *to* יְהוָה.   B1
Feast of Booths
⁴¹אַתֶּם *are to celebrate it as a* חַג לַיהוָה *for seven* יָמִים *in the* שָׁנָה. *It is a statute forever throughout your generations—you are to celebrate it in the seventh* חֹדֶשׁ. ⁴²אַתֶּם *are to dwell in* _____ *for seven* יָמִים. *All the native-born in* יִשְׂרָאֵל *are to live in* סֻכּוֹת, *booths* ⁴³ *so that your generations may know that I had* בְּנֵי יִשְׂרָאֵל *to dwell in* סֻכּוֹת *when I brought them out of the land of Egypt. I am* יְהוָה *your* אֱלֹהִים.'"

Although many people call this מוֹעֵד the "Feast of Tabernacles," the word סֻכּוֹת refers to   B2
modest, temporary structures (like huts used for farm animals) that provide shade and covering. סֻכּוֹת does not refer to the beauty and holiness of the original Tabernacle which Moses and the Israelites built in the wilderness..

What does it mean to "dwell" in a סֻכָּה? The עִבְרִית root for "dwell" is יָשַׁב meaning sit,   B3
remain, abide or dwell. Hence the tradition worldwide is to sit and eat in the סֻכָּה.

סֻכּוֹת in Israel   B4

In certain religious communities throughout יִשְׂרָאֵל, elaborate wood סֻכּוֹת are built big enough to eat and sleep for the entire week. In Tiberias, near the Sea of Galilee, my husband and I had the privilege of having a traditional סֻכּוֹת meal inside one of these סֻכּוֹת, complete with a bed, dining table and electricity!

To see a heart-warming, modern-day example of סֻכּוֹת, watch the Israeli movie "Ushpizin" (meaning "guests").

During סֻכּוֹת, we are commanded to leave the comforts of our home to dwell in temporary   B5
סֻכּוֹת to remember the challenges of our ancestors in the desert and the faithfulness of
יְהוָה to deliver them. These are some of the traditions associated with this command.

- It is customary to begin building the סֻכָּה immediately after יוֹם הַכִּפֻּרִים ends.
  These are built in backyards, streets, gardens and even on balconies!
- The Rabbinic customs for building a סֻכָּה are that it must have at least three walls and
  the ceiling must provide shade during the יוֹם yet allow the stars to be seen at night.
  Traditionally, fresh palm branches are used to cover the top.
- In some Jewish homes, the סֻכָּה comes right out of a box, and is built with metal poles
  and nylon walls (much like a camping tent). Some come with bamboo ceilings and
  include doors and windows.
- Decorating the סֻכָּה is a family event. Fresh and artificial פְּרִי, paper chains, pictures,
  lights, and ornaments are attached to the walls and hung from the ceiling.
- Throughout the seven _____ of the חַג, all meals are eaten in the סֻכָּה, and
  <small>days</small>
  guests are encouraged to come to visit. Even restaurants build their own סֻכּוֹת!
- Throughout this מוֹעֵד, food gifts are given to the poor.

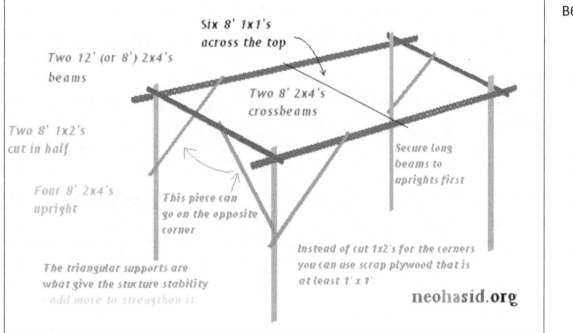

B6

We used this simple סֻכָּה design to build large סֻכּוֹת in Tennessee and Colorado, USA.   B7
(See picture on next page.) Thanks to Rabbi Seidenberg for permission to post.
http://www.neohasid.org/sukkot/a_simple_sukkah/

The First Thanksgiving?   B8

סֻכּוֹת may very well have been the original Thanksgiving חַג marking the end of the
קָצִיר season. Some people believe that the first Thanksgiving celebrated by the
Pilgrims in America was a סֻכּוֹת remembrance!

C - Feast of the Ingathering

Exodus 34:22: "אַתָּה are to observe חַג שָׁבוּעוֹת, which is the בִּכּוּרִים of the wheat   C1
_____ , as well as חַג הָאָסִיף (khag ha-a-SEEF) "Feast of Ingathering" at the turn
harvest
of the שָׁנָה."

Leviticus 23:39: "On the fifteenth יוֹם of the seventh חֹדֶשׁ, when you have gathered in   C2
the פְּרִי of the land, אַתָּה are to keep the חַג לַיהוָה for seven יָמִים. The first יוֹם is
to be a שַׁבָּת rest, and the eighth יוֹם will also be a שַׁבָּת rest."

D – Hebrew Root שׂ.מ.ח

Fill in the missing words, then circle the root letters in all of the Hebrew words below.

Words from the Root		Root Meaning	Root
joy			שׂ.מ.ח
	שִׂמְחַת	joyful, rejoice	used 152 X In the Scriptures
joyful, happy			
our joy	שִׂמְחָתֵנוּ		

E - Season (time) of our Joy זְמַן שִׂמְחָתֵנוּ

Deuteronomy 16:13-15: *"¹³You are to keep* חַג הַסֻּכּוֹת *for seven* יָמִים *after gathering in* **E1**
the produce from your threshing floor and winepress. ¹⁴ *So you will rejoice in your* חַג—*you,*
your son and daughter, slave and maid, Levite and outsider, orphan and widow within your
gates. ¹⁵ *Seven* יָמִים *you will feast to* יְהֹוָה *your* אֱלֹהִים *in the place He chooses,*
because יְהֹוָה *your* אֱלֹהִים *will bless you in all your produce and in all the work of your*
hand, and you will be _____*."*
joyful

סֻכּוֹת is a joyful remembrance of the goodness of יְהֹוָה as He protected His chosen **E2**
people, _____ , traveling through the desert wilderness on the way
Israel
to the Promised Land.

Waving the לוּלָב and the אֶתְרוֹג **E3**

Leviticus 23:40: *"On the first* יוֹם *you are to take choice* פְּרִי *of*
trees, branches of palm trees, boughs of leafy trees, and willows
of the brook, and rejoice before יְהֹוָה *your* אֱלֹהִים.

From the Scripture above, the Rabbinic tradition is to joyfully wave the לוּלָב and the **E4**
אֶתְרוֹג both in the סֻכָּה and during Synagogue services.

The לוּלָב (meaning "date palm frond") is also the traditional name given to the **E5**
collection of branches including a date palm, 2 myrtle branches and 2 willow
branches, all tied together. (Nehemiah 8:15 includes the "myrtle" branch.)

The אֶתְרוֹג is a citron (a citrus fruit found in Israel) which represents פְּרִי. **E6**

Traditionally the לוּלָב and אֶתְרוֹג are held together and waved in six directions **E7**
(east, south, west, north, up and down) to convey that the קָדוֹשׁ presence of יְהֹוָה
is over the whole world. The motions also symbolize that we are to bear טוֹב
_____ , do טוֹב deeds, and grow closer to יְהֹוָה and His קָדוֹשׁ Word.
fruit

You can purchase a לוּלָב and אֶתְרוֹג directly from יִשְׂרָאֵל or you can create one of **E8**
your own! Find the branches listed in E5 above (if they are available in your area) or
use local branches to represent the לוּלָב. A lemon can substitute for an אֶתְרוֹג.

In Psalm 100:2, fill in the missing English words, then use syllable lines and   E9
cantillation marks to help אַתָּה pronounce the עִבְרִית.

בְּשִׂמְחָה   אֶת־יְהֹוָה   עִבְדוּ

with _____   _____   serve/work for/worship

---

*The root for "serve," ע.ב.ד also means "work" and "worship". Everything   E10
we do in חַיִּים, as we work, serve or worship, should always be our very
best effort for our wonderful יְהֹוָה...and it should be done with שִׂמְחָה!*

F - Word Pairs - סְמִיכוּת

In English, we often put two nouns together to make a new single concept.   F1
Examples are "goldfish," "seat belt," and "water fountain."

עִבְרִית also uses word pairs (called "constructs" in English) which are called סְמִיכוּת   F2
(smee-KHOOT). Many of these סְמִיכוּת are found in the מוֹעֲדִים Scriptures.

Examples: בְּנֵי יִשְׂרָאֵל   חַג הַסֻּכּוֹת   F3

Israel **of** sons/   the booths **of** holiday
children

Notice that in most word pairs, the word "**of**" must be added to translate correctly.   F4
Often, the vowels and letters will change in the first word of the pair.
You can learn more about "word pairs" in *Biblical Hebrew with Joy!* Lesson 7.

Write the English or Hebrew meaning of the following word pairs.

	יוֹם הַכִּפֻּרִים	F5
	אֱלֹהֵי יִשְׂרָאֵל	F6
	שִׂמְחַת תּוֹרָה	F7
	בְּנֵי יִשְׂרָאֵל	F8
	שַׁבָּת שָׁלוֹם	F9

G- Eighth Day Assembly

Leviticus 23:36: *"The eighth יוֹם will be a מִקְרָא־קֹדֶשׁ to you, and you are to bring an offering by אֵשׁ to יְהוָה. It is a solemn assembly —you should לֹא do laborious מְלָאכָה."* G1

The eighth שְׁמִינִי (sh-mee-NEE) יוֹם of סֻכּוֹת is to include an assembly עֲצֶרֶת (a-**TSE**-ret) and it must be observed as a שַׁבָּת. This day ends the joyful חַג הַסֻּכּוֹת. In יִשְׂרָאֵל, this eighth יוֹם is combined with שִׂמְחַת תּוֹרָה (see H1 below). G2

The number eight holds special importance in the Word of אֱלֹהִים. If seven symbolizes perfection and completion, eight goes beyond to usher in new beginnings! G3

Eighth יוֹם In Biblical History G4

Solomon dedicated his Temple on שְׁמִינִי עֲצֶרֶת (the 8th day assembly of סֻכּוֹת).
"On the eighth יוֹם they held a solemn assembly, for they had celebrated the dedication of the altar for seven יָמִים and the feast for seven יָמִים."
2 Chronicles 7:9

In the time of Nehemiah, the people celebrated their redemption from captivity during סֻכּוֹת and the eighth יוֹם: *"So they kept the festival for seven יָמִים, and on the eighth יוֹם, according to the regulation, there was a solemn assembly."*
Nehemiah 8:18

H - Joy of Torah שִׂמְחַת תּוֹרָה

שִׂמְחַת תּוֹרָה is celebrated on the eighth יוֹם of סֻכּוֹת in Israel. (In some communities in the Diaspora (outside of יִשְׂרָאֵל), a ninth יוֹם is added. During this holiday of _____ (joy), the תּוֹרָה scroll readings are finished for the שָׁנָה and the תּוֹרָה is rolled back to the beginning (Gen. 1:1), which starts a new yearly תּוֹרָה cycle. The men dance around the תּוֹרָה, the children throw candy, and the תּוֹרָה is carried through the neighborhood, followed by the שָׂמֵחַ congregation. It is indeed a celebration of the שִׂמְחָה of the קָדוֹשׁ Word of אֱלֹהִים. H1

en.Wikipedia.org

I – Dancing for שִׂמְחָה

Another form of שִׂמְחָה before _____ is dancing. Just as David danced before   I1
יְהוָה to worship Him, we can also praise and worship our amazing Father by dancing.
_{LORD}

Below, Jackie Newman of BShem Hebraic Dance Ministry shares beautiful סֻכּוֹת   I2
dances with us. To view her YouTube channel, scan the QR code below or go to
youtube.com/channel/UCygOyqRF5ebp5r4-e0ZCgng

J - Shehecheyanu שֶׁהֶחֱיָנוּ Prayer

As we complete the eighth day of סֻכּוֹת, we have also completed the entire מוֹעֲדִים   J1
cycle from Leviticus 23 and we begin a fresh new cycle. It is therefore fitting that we end
with the שֶׁהֶחֱיָנוּ prayer as יְהוָה has indeed "kept us alive" through the entire cycle!

אַתָּה will recognize the first line as the בְּרָכָה from Lesson **3.** Write the English   J2
meaning below each word. On the second line, draw syllable lines then read the
entire prayer out loud.

בָּרוּךְ   אַתָּה   יְהוָה   אֱלֹהֵינוּ   מֶלֶךְ   הָעוֹלָם   J3
_____   _____   _____   _____   _____   _____

שֶׁהֶחֱיָנוּ   וְקִיְּמָנוּ   וְהִגִּיעָנוּ   לִזְמַן   הַזֶּה   J4

| this | to time | and brought us | and sustained us | kept us alive |

Blessed (are) You, LORD our GOD, King (of) the universe,   J5
who has kept us alive, and sustained us and brought us to this
season (time).

8 – Feast of Booths Exercises   שֵׁם _____

1. Read and translate the following Hebrew words.

שִׂמְחָה קָדוֹשׁ אֶתְרוֹג חֹדֶשׁ בְּנֵי שָׁנָה אֵשׁ סֻכּוֹת קֹדֶשׁ

מִקְרָא סֻכָּה נֶפֶשׁ לוּלָב שִׂמְחַת יִשְׂרָאֵל פְּרִי שָׁבוּעוֹת זִכָּרוֹן

Fill in the missing Hebrew root or English meanings for the following <u>roots</u>.

	ר.א.שׁ	.2
new, renew		.3
	מ.ל.ךְ	.4
cover, protect		.5
	שׁ.ב.ע	.6

7. סֻכּוֹת is also called the "Season of our Joy". Write this in Hebrew below.

_____

8. From Deuteronomy 16:13-15, circle the words you know (many have prefixes or suffixes attached.) You should find at least 12 words from this book.

13 חַג הַסֻּכֹּת תַּעֲשֶׂה לְךָ שִׁבְעַת יָמִים בְּאָסְפְּךָ מִגָּרְנְךָ וּמִיִּקְבֶךָ:

14 וְשָׂמַחְתָּ בְּחַגֶּךָ אַתָּה וּבִנְךָ וּבִתֶּךָ וְעַבְדְּךָ וַאֲמָתֶךָ וְהַלֵּוִי וְהַגֵּר וְהַיָּתוֹם וְהָאַלְמָנָה אֲשֶׁר בִּשְׁעָרֶיךָ:

15 שִׁבְעַת יָמִים תָּחֹג לַיהוָה אֱלֹהֶיךָ בַּמָּקוֹם אֲשֶׁר־יִבְחַר יְהוָה כִּי יְבָרֶכְךָ יְהוָה אֱלֹהֶיךָ בְּכֹל תְּבוּאָתְךָ וּבְכֹל מַעֲשֵׂה יָדֶיךָ וְהָיִיתָ אַךְ שָׂמֵחַ:

9. Write the <u>root</u> meanings of שׂ.מ.ח.

_____

10. There are three different names for this holiday: Feast of Booths, Feast of the Ingathering and the Season of Our Joy. Write all three in עִבְרִית.

a. _____

b. _____

c. _____

83

Write the English meaning of the following סְמִיכוּת (word pairs).

	בְּנֵי יִשְׂרָאֵל	11.
	חַג הַסֻכּוֹת	12.
	שִׂמְחַת תּוֹרָה	13.
	אֱלֹהֵי יִשְׂרָאֵל	14.

15. Using Hebrew and English, write a prayer to יְהֹוָה thanking Him for סֻכּוֹת. (See page 74 for an example.) Use as many עִבְרִית words as possible:

_____

_____

_____

_____

_____

_____

_____

_____

_____

9 - Feast of Dedication חֲנֻכָּה

> חַג חֲנֻכָּה שָׂמֵחַ!

A – Vocabulary

Memorize the following Hebrew words used in this lesson.

English	Gender	Transliteration	Hebrew	
7-branched lamp stand	*fs*	m-no-RA	מְנוֹרָה	A1
9-branched lamp stand	*fs*	kha-noo-kee-**YA**	חֲנֻכִּיָּה	A2
caretaker	*ms*	sha-MASH	שַׁמָּשׁ	A3
dedication	*fs*	kha-noo-KA	חֲנֻכָּה	A4
Judah	*ms*	y-hoo-DA	יְהוּדָה	A5
light	*ms*	or	אוֹר	A6
miracle	*ms*	nes	נֵס	A7
night	*ms*	**LAI**-la	לַיְלָה	A8
oil	*ms*	**SHE**-men	שֶׁמֶן	A9
salvation	*fs*	y-shoo-A	יְשׁוּעָה	A10

A11

The Miracle of חֲנֻכָּה

Although חֲנֻכָּה is not listed in Leviticus 23 as a מוֹעֵד of יְהוָה, it is a significant historical חַג for the Jewish people. The story of יְהוּדָה Macabee and his tiny band defeating the huge Syrian army reveals the miraculous יְשׁוּעָה of יְהוָה. This incredible miracle is reflected in the following traditional prayer recited each night of חֲנֻכָּה while lighting the חֲנֻכִּיָּה:

בָּרוּךְ אַתָּה יְהוָה אֱלֹהֵינוּ מֶלֶךְ הָעוֹלָם, שֶׁעָשָׂה נִסִּים לַאֲבוֹתֵינוּ בַּיָּמִים הָהֵם בַּזְּמַן הַזֶּה.

ba-ROOKH a-TA a-do-NAI e-lo-HAY-noo **ME**-lech ha-o-LAM, she-a-SA nee-SEEM la-a-vo-**TAY**-noo ba-ya-MEEM ha-HEM baz-MAN ha-ZE

Blessed are You, LORD our GOD, King of the Universe, who has accomplished miracles for our fathers in those days at this season.

B – Story of חֲנֻכָּה

During the 2nd century B.C., יִשְׂרָאֵל came under the control of a Syrian king, Antiochus Epiphanes, who outlawed Judaism and ordered the Jews to worship Greek gods. His soldiers killed thousands of people in Jerusalem and desecrated the Second Temple by building an altar to Zeus and sacrificing pigs.   **B1**

Mattathias, a Jewish priest, and his five sons, rebelled against Antiochus. When Mattathias died, his son יְהוּדָה, known as יְהוּדָה the "Maccabee," became the new leader. Within two years, the Jews successfully drove the Syrians out of Jerusalem, using what may have been the first "guerilla warfare."   **B2**

יְהוּדָה immediately called upon his followers to cleanse the temple and rededicate it to יְהוָה. (This is why the חַג is called חֲנֻכָּה.) Truly, a great נֵס happened there! With the help of יְהוָה, the tiny band of Jewish warriors defeated the huge Syrian army! Although the story of חֲנֻכָּה (meaning _____) does not appear in the תּוֹרָה (as the events occurred after it was written), it is found in the books of 1st and 2nd Maccabees.   **B3**

B4

> ## Why was יְהוּדָה called "Maccabee"?
>
> Some believe that מַכַּבִּי (ma-ka-BEE) comes from the Hebrew word for
> "hammer" מַקֶּב (ma-KEV) symbolizing strength and power.
> Others say it is based on an acronym meaning
> "Who is like Adonai, among the gods?" (Exodus 15:11).
>
> מִי־ כָמֹכָה בָּאֵלִם יְהוָה
> who   is like   among the gods   Adonai

1st Maccabees 4:52-53, 56, 59 (NCB)   **B5**

52 Early in the morning on the twenty-fifth יוֹם of the ninth חֹדֶשׁ, which is the חֹדֶשׁ of Kislev, in the one hundred forty-eighth שָׁנָה, 53 they rose and offered sacrifice.. 56 So they celebrated the חֲנֻכָּה of the altar for eight יָמִים, and joyfully offered burnt offerings; they offered a sacrifice of well-being and a thanksgiving offering. 59 Then יְהוּדָה and his brothers and all the assembly of יִשְׂרָאֵל determined that every שָׁנָה at that season the יָמִים of חֲנֻכָּה of the altar should be observed with שִׂמְחָה and gladness for eight יָמִים, beginning with the twenty-fifth יוֹם of the _____ of Kislev.
month

2nd Maccabees 10:6-7 (NCB)　B6

⁶ The celebration and rejoicing lasted for eight יָמִים, in the manner of the סֻכּוֹת, as they recalled how, only a short time before, during the סֻכּוֹת, they had been living like wild animals in the mountains and caves. ⁷ And so, carrying wands entwined with ivy, and leafy branches and לוּלָב, they offered hymns of thanksgiving to Him whose guiding hand had enabled them to achieve the purification of His קָדוֹשׁ place.

From 2nd Maccabees above, why did the Jews celebrate חֲנֻכָּה for eight יָמִים?　B7

B8

> ## Train up a Child!
> Proverbs 22:6
> *"Train up a child in the way he should go, when he is old he will not turn from it."*
> In this Scripture, the עִבְרִית word for "train up" is the word חֲנֹךְ (kha-NOKH)
> from the root ח.נ.ךְ, the same root as חֲנֻכָּה! Not only are we to "train up" a
> child, but we are to "dedicate" him (or her) to our awesome יְהֹוָה!

י.ד.ה Root עִבְרִית – C

Fill in the missing word, then circle the root letters in all of the Hebrew words below.

Words from the Root		Root Meaning	Root
Judah, praised			
thanks	תּוֹדָה	praise, give thanks	י.ד.ה
Jew, Jewish	יְהוּדִי		used 932X
hand (used to praise יְהֹוָה)	יָד		In the Scriptures

D – The Feast of Lights

Another beautiful שֵׁם for this חַג is חַג הָאוּרִים (khag ha-oo-REEM) "The Feast of Lights." D1
The שֵׁם comes from the legend of the נֵס of the שֶׁמֶן. According to the story, after cleansing
and rededicating the Temple, there was only enough שֶׁמֶן to last for one לַיְלָה. Miraculously,
the מְנוֹרָה stayed lit for eight יָמִים, leaving enough time to find a fresh supply of
_____. Thus, we light the _____ on each of the nights of חֲנֻכָּה.
oil   9-branched lamp stand

The Beauty of אוֹר   D2

The Hebrew word אוֹר, has depths of meaning that can be life-transforming. It conveys
illumination, as in a bright clear day, but it also means the אוֹר of תּוֹרָה.

His lamp (to our feet) shines where our feet are standing today and His אוֹר (to our path)
illuminates what's up ahead on the road, present and future!
(Deb Wiley, *Ears to Hear*)

Psalm 119:105 *"Your word is a lamp to my feet and a אוֹר to my path."*

Psalm 27:1 that *"The LORD (Himself!) is my אוֹר and my יְשׁוּעָה. Whom shall I fear?"*

Psalm 119:130 *"The entrance of your Word brings אוֹר!"*

E – י Suffix

Fill in the missing Hebrew and English words below.

אִירָא	מִמִּי	וְיִשְׁעִי	אוֹרִי		תְּהִלִּים 27:1	E1
shall I fear	from whom	_____ my _____	(is) my _____	LORD	_____ 27:1	
					Normal English	

Look at these words from the Scripture above noting the י suffix. E2

י + יְשׁוּעָה + וְ = וְיִשְׁעִי   י + אוֹר = אוֹרִי
my   salvation   and   my   light

In most cases, the י suffix signifies "my" or "me" and applies to either a man or woman E3
(first person is not gender specific). Remember that vowels and/or letters may be added,
changed, or dropped when adding a suffix.

Write the English meaning of the words below. Remember to use "my" or "me." E4
תּוֹרָתִי _____   נַפְשִׁי _____

You can learn more about Hebrew suffixes in *Biblical Hebrew with Joy!* Lessons 5, 8 & 9.

F – Traditions and Celebrations of וְחֲנֻכָּה

Lighting the חֲנֻכִּיָּה   F1

Although the Biblical מְנוֹרָה has seven branches, a חֲנֻכִּיָּה with nine branches is used during חֲנֻכָּה. On the first לַיְלָה, a special candle called a שַׁמָּשׁ is lit first. (This candle is different from the others, usually placed higher on the חֲנֻכִּיָּה.) The שַׁמָּשׁ then lights the first candle. On the second לַיְלָה, the שַׁמָּשׁ lights two candles and the pattern continues throughout the eight nights.

In Israel, many families encourage each member to have their own   F2
חֲנֻכִּיָּה, many being home-made. On the first לַיְלָה of חֲנֻכָּה, families gather in their homes to light the candles, recite traditional prayers and sing their favorite _____ songs.

 dedication

Giving Gifts   F3

A common tradition in America is to give a small gift for every לַיְלָה of the eight-יוֹם _____. (Growing up in a Jewish home, I loved this part of the holiday!)

 holiday
In יִשְׂרָאֵל, however, this is not part of the tradition!

Spinning the Dreidel   F4

In America, Jewish children play the Dreidel (**DRAY**-del) game. "Dreidel" is a Yiddish word meaning "spinning top." The Hebrew word is סְבִיבוֹן (s-vee-VON). The four Hebrew letters on the dreidel are an acronym for "A Great נֵס Happened THERE."

שָׁם	הָיָה	גָּדוֹל	נֵס
sham	ha-YA	ga-DOL	nes
there	happened	great	miracle

In Israel, the last letter, שׁ, changes to a פ representing פֹּה (here) because "A Great נֵס happened HERE!"

According to tradition, Jews would hide their study by playing with a dreidel (sometimes   F5
in caves!). If the Syrian soldiers burst into the forbidden study groups, they would see a group of gamblers instead of scholars studying the _____.

 instruction

Dreidel Game   F6

Each player starts with 5 coins and puts one coin in the center of the table for the "pot". One at a time, each player spins the dreidel and must do what the letter suggests (see below.) Before each turn, all players put one coin in the pot. Play until one person has all the coins OR play for 10 minutes, then the player with the most coins wins the pot.

נ   Nun – takes "none" of the pot

ג   Gimmel – "gimmy" all of the pot

ה   Hay -takes "half" of the pot

ש   Shin - put one "in" to the pot

Eating Fried Foods   F7

To remember the נֵס of the שֶׁמֶן, traditional חֲנֻכָּה foods are fried in שֶׁמֶן. The favorite dish is "Latkes" (pronounced **LAT**-kuz), a Yiddish word meaning potato pancakes.

Easy Potato Latkes   F8

Makes 10-12 large or 20 to 24 small latkes

Ingredients
8 cups frozen shredded hash browns
¼ Cup grated onion
6 Eggs, beaten
½ Cup all-purpose flour
1 tsp salt
2 cups Vegetable oil
Sour cream and Applesauce

Directions
1. Thaw the potatoes, then wring out well with paper towels, extracting as much moisture as possible.
2. In a medium bowl stir the potatoes, onion, eggs, flour and salt together.
3. In a large heavy-bottomed skillet over medium-high heat, heat the oil until hot. Place large spoonfuls of the potato mixture into the hot oil, pressing down on them to form 1/4 to 1/2 inch thick patties. Brown on one side, turn and brown on the other. Let drain on paper towels.
4. Serve hot with sour cream and applesauce on the side.

9 – Feast of Dedication Exercises שֵׁם _____

1. Read and translate the following Hebrew words.

שִׂמְחָה חֲנֻכָּה לַיְלָה חֹדֶשׁ יְהוּדָה שָׁנָה שֶׁמֶן מְנוֹרָה חֶסֶד
חֲנֻכִּיָּה יְשׁוּעָה אוֹר שָׁבוּעוֹת חֵטְא חַיִּים מִקְרָא סֻכָּה שֶׁמֶשׁ נֵס

From this lesson, fill in the עִבְרִית and English words for the following <u>mixed-up letters</u>.

English	עִבְרִית	
		.2 דְּיְהוּה
		.3 יְכָּהחַנֻ
		.4 מֶןשֶׁ
		.5 יהלָלַ
		.6 וּנהרָמְ
		.7 רוֹא
		.8 סֵנ
		.9 כָּחֲדהנֻ

10. חֲנֻכָּה is also called the "Festival of Lights". Write this in Hebrew below.

_____

11. Write the <u>root</u> meanings of ה.ד.ר: _____

12. Write two עִבְרִית words that come from this root.

_____   _____

13. What is the English meaning of the following words?

יִשְׁעִי   אוֹרִי   נַפְשִׁי   תּוֹרָתִי

_____ _____ _____ _____

_____ _____ _____ _____

Read the following Scriptures out loud. They proclaim the אוֹר of יְהוָה and His miraculous יְשׁוּעָה. Circle the words אַתָּה know and draw syllable lines to help you pronounce each word correctly. Then, write the English translation.

.14   Genesis 1:5

וַיִּקְרָא אֱלֹהִים לָאוֹר יוֹם וְלַחֹשֶׁךְ קָרָא לָיְלָה

_____English

_____

.15   Psalm 18:28 (29)

כִּי־אַתָּה תָּאִיר נֵרִי יְהוָה אֱלֹהַי יַגִּיהַּ חָשְׁכִּי:

_____Engish

_____

.16   Psalm 118:14

עָזִּי וְזִמְרָת יָהּ וַיְהִי־לִּי לִישׁוּעָה:

_____Engish

_____

10 - Feast of Lots פּוּרִים

חַג פּוּרִים שָׂמֵחַ!

A – Vocabulary

Memorize the following Hebrew words used in this lesson.

English	Gender	Transliteration	Hebrew	
Ahasuerus (Xerxes)	ms	a-khash-ve-ROSH	אֲחַשְׁוֵרוֹשׁ	A1
Esther	fs	es-TER	אֶסְתֵּר	A2
Hadassah	fs	ha-da-SA	הֲדַסָּה	A3
Haman	ms	ha-MAN	הָמָן	A4
Jews	mpl	y-hoo-DEEM	יְהוּדִים	A5
lot (to cast)	ms	poor	פּוּר	A6
lots	mpl	poo-REEM	פּוּרִים	A7
Mordecai*	ms	mor-do-KHAI*	מָרְדְּכַי	A8
scroll	fs	m-gee-LA	מְגִילָה	A9
Vashti	fs	vash-TEE	וַשְׁתִּי	A10

*◌ָ usually has the "ah" sound, but it can sometimes have the long "o" sound.   A11

(all) kol = כָּל   (Mordecai) mor-do-KHAI = מָרְדְּכַי

Why Celebrate פּוּרִים?   A12

פּוּרִים is a Biblical חַג containing an abundance of prophetic revelation for all people devoted to the אֱלֹהִים of יִשְׂרָאֵל and His people. Unlike the other מוֹעֲדִים of the LORD, this חַג is not commanded in the book of Leviticus 23. Rather, it is a special time which מָרְדְּכַי commanded the Jewish people to celebrate for all generations as a remembrance of when אֱלֹהִים turned their sorrow into שִׂמְחָה and their mourning into dancing. Hallelujah!

Adapted from Hannah Nesher, VoiceforIsrael.net

B – Scriptures from אֶסְתֵּר

B1 פּוּרִים is the one חַג that has an entire Biblical book devoted to it. If you've never read the book of אֶסְתֵּר, read it now to understand the beautiful story of יְשׁוּעָה for the LORD's chosen people, the יְהוּדִים. Then, read the following key verses from this incredible book.

B2 Esther 1:1-2 *"This is what happened in the days of אֲחַשְׁוֵרוֹשׁ, the אֲחַשְׁוֵרוֹשׁ who reigned over 127 provinces from India to Ethiopia. At that time King אֲחַשְׁוֵרוֹשׁ sat on his royal throne in the castle in Shushan (Susa)."*

B3 Esther 1:12 *"But Queen וַשְׁתִּי refused to come at the king's command conveyed by the eunuchs. Then the _____ became furious and burned with anger."*
<u>king</u>

B4 Esther 2:5, 7, 17 *"There was a Jewish man in the Shushan palace whose name was מָרְדֳּכַי. He had raised הֲדַסָּה — that is אֶסְתֵּר — his uncle's daughter, for she had neither father nor mother. Now the מֶלֶךְ loved אֶסְתֵּר more than all the other women, and she won his grace and favor more than all the other virgins. So he placed the royal crown upon her head and made her queen instead of וַשְׁתִּי."*

B5 Esther 3:5, 6, 7 *"When הָמָן saw that מָרְדֳּכַי was not bowing down or paying him honor, הָמָן was filled with rage. So הָמָן sought to destroy all the יְהוּדִים, the people of מָרְדֳּכַי, who were throughout the whole kingdom of אֲחַשְׁוֵרוֹשׁ. In the first month (that is the חֹדֶשׁ of Nisan), in the twelfth year of King אֲחַשְׁוֵרוֹשׁ, they cast the פּוּר (that is, "the lot") in the presence of הָמָן from יוֹם to יוֹם and חֹדֶשׁ to חֹדֶשׁ, up to the twelfth חֹדֶשׁ, which is the _____ of Adar."*
<u>month</u>

B6 Esther 4:13-14 *"מָרְדֳּכַי told them to reply to אֶסְתֵּר with this answer, "Do not think in your נֶפֶשׁ that you will escape in the king's household more than all the יְהוּדִים. For if you remain silent at this time, relief and deliverance will arise for the יְהוּדִים from another place—but you and your father's house will perish. Who knows whether you have attained royal status for such a time as this?"*

B7 Esther 4:15-16 *"אֶסְתֵּר sent this to reply to מָרְדֳּכַי, "Go! Gather together all the יְהוּדִים who are in Shushan and fast for me. Do not eat or drink for three יָמִים, night or יוֹם. My maids and I will fast in the same way. Afterwards, I will go in to the מֶלֶךְ, even though it is not according to the law. So if I perish, I perish!"*

Esther 8:5-6 *"She said, "If it pleases the מֶלֶךְ, and if I have found favor before him and it* **B8**
seems right to the מֶלֶךְ, and if I am pleasing in his eyes, let an edict be written rescinding the
dispatches devised by הָמָן, the son of Hammedatha the Agagite, which he wrote to destroy
the יְהוּדִים who are throughout the king's provinces. For how can I endure seeing the
disaster that will fall on my people? How can I bear to see the destruction of my relatives?"

Esther 8:7 *"King אֲחַשְׁוֵרוֹשׁ said to Queen אֶסְתֵּר and מָרְדֳּכַי the Jew, "I have given the* **B9**
estate of הָמָן to _____ *and had him hanged on the gallows, because he*
Esther
stretched out his hand against the יְהוּדִים."

Esther 8:11-12 *"The מֶלֶךְ granted the right for יְהוּדִים in every city to assemble themselves* **B10**
and to protect themselves—to destroy, kill, and annihilate any army of any people or province
that might attack them and their women and children, and to plunder their possessions. The
יוֹם appointed for this in all the provinces of King אֲחַשְׁוֵרוֹשׁ was the thirteenth יוֹם of the
twelfth חֹדֶשׁ, the חֹדֶשׁ of Adar."

Esther 9:1 *"Consequently, on the thirteenth יוֹם of the twelfth חֹדֶשׁ (that is the חֹדֶשׁ* **B11**
of Adar), the king's edict and his law drew near to be carried out. On that day the enemies of
the _____ *had hoped to overpower them, but contrary to expectations the*
Jews
יְהוּדִים gained the upper hand over those that hated them."

Esther 9:20-22 *"מָרְדֳּכַי recorded these events and he sent letters to all the יְהוּדִים* **B12**
throughout the provinces of King אֲחַשְׁוֵרוֹשׁ, both near and far, urging them to celebrate the
fourteenth and fifteenth יָמִים of Adar every שָׁנָה as the יָמִים when the יְהוּדִים got relief
from their enemies, and as the חֹדֶשׁ when their sorrow was turned into שִׂמְחָה and their
mourning into celebration."

C – עִבְרִית Root ס.ת.ר

Fill in the missing word, then (circle) the root letters in the עִבְרִית words below.

Words from the Root		Root Meaning	Root	
Esther (Persian meaning: "star")		hide, conceal	**ס.ת.ר** used 137X In the Scriptures	**C1**
hidden (Genesis 4:14)	אֶסְתֵּר			
hide (Deuteronomy 31:18)	אַסְתִּיר			

The Hidden אֱלֹהִים   C2

Powerful חַיִּים lessons have been hidden within the Book of אֶסְתֵּר, one of which
involves "secret or hidden identities." The very name אֶסְתֵּר comes from a root
ס.ת.ר meaning "hidden or concealed." It appears in the תּוֹרָה in the עִבְרִית
phrase, "I will hide (אַסְתִּיר) My Face" (Deut. 31:18). Even אֱלֹהִים is hidden
in the story. The closest reference to אֱלֹהִים is when מָרְדְּכַי tells אֶסְתֵּר that
redemption for the _____ will come from "another place."
                              Jews

Even when אֱלֹהִים seems hidden from us, He is still there, for He has promised to
never leave us nor forsake us. He is "Imanu" (with us) El (God) – אֱלֹהִים with us.
Even when we cannot see nor understand what is going on
in our lives, with enemies before us, behind us, and surrounding us, אֱלֹהִים
is still there, even if hidden, but faithfully working behind the scenes to work
out all the details, divine appointments, and circumstances to secure our victory.
He may even ask for our participation in the drama!

Hannah Nesher   VoiceforIsrael.net

In Esther 4:14, מָרְדְּכַי challenges אֶסְתֵּר to speak to the מֶלֶךְ and reveal her hidden   C3
Jewish identity. Below, <u>add syllable lines</u>, then read this challenge out loud.

וּמִי   יוֹדֵעַ   אִם   לְעֵת   כָּזֹאת   הִגַּעַתְּ   לַמַּלְכוּת

to the kingdom	you have come	as this	for a time	if	knows	and who

For more reading practice, read the rest of Esther 4:14 (don't forget syllable lines).

כִּי אִם־הַחֲרֵשׁ תַּחֲרִישִׁי בָּעֵת הַזֹּאת רֶוַח וְהַצָּלָה יַעֲמוֹד   C4

לַיְּהוּדִים מִמָּקוֹם אַחֵר וְאַתְּ וּבֵית־אָבִיךְ תֹּאבֵדוּ וּמִי יוֹדֵעַ   C5

אִם־לְעֵת כָּזֹאת הִגַּעַתְּ לַמַּלְכוּת: C6

"For if you remain silent at this time, relief and deliverance will arise for the יְהוּדִים   C7
from another place—but you and your father's house will perish. Who knows whether
you have attained royal status for such a time as this?"

D– Traditions and Celebrations of פּוּרִים

פּוּרִים Costumes   D1

The concept of concealed, hidden or mistaken identities is a theme throughout the Book of אֶסְתֵּר and Feast of פּוּרִים. Traditionally, costumes and masks are worn to disguise identities. Many communities have elaborate parades where prizes are awarded for the best _____ character costume.

lots

פּוּרִים Surprise   D2

In 2003, my sister Pam, her husband and three young teenagers immigrated to יִשְׂרָאֵל (in עִבְרִית this is called, "Making Aliyah"). When they arrived in March at the Tel Aviv airport, they were shocked to see young people with purple hair and wild costumes. They had no idea that this was an Israeli פּוּרִים custom! As of the writing of this book, Pam and her family have been in the Promised Land for almost twenty years, and they now have many Israeli grandkids celebrating פּוּרִים each שָׁנָה!

פּוּרִים Plays   D3

פּוּרִים plays are also a favorite tradition where the children all take a part as a Biblical character from the story. When the name "אֶסְתֵּר" is spoken, the audience all blow noisemakers, clap and say, "YAY!" When the name "הָמָן" is mentioned, they all shout a loud, "BOO!"

Queen אֶסְתֵּר   D4

Every שָׁנָה growing up, our synagogue, Temple Beth שָׁלוֹם, held auditions for the פּוּרִים play. And every שָׁנָה, I yearned to play Queen אֶסְתֵּר. Sadly, every שָׁנָה, when the cast was announced, I was selected to play מָרְדְּכַי (since we did not have enough boys willing to be in the play!)

Then, a miracle happened! A few years ago, as an adult, I finally had a chance to dress up as Queen אֶסְתֵּר. It was the highlight of my חַג!

Gifts for the Poor D5

During פּוּרִים, gift baskets are given to the poor based on Esther 9:22: *"These were to be days of feasting, celebration and sending presents of food to one another and giving gifts to the poor."* The traditional cookies in these baskets are called "Hamentaschen," a Yiddish word meaning "Haman's Pockets." The עִבְרִית words are אָזְנֵי־הָמָן (oz-NAY ha-MAN) meaning "Haman's ears!"

Easy Hamentaschen Recipe D6

- 2/3 cup butter or margarine
- 1/2 cup sugar
- 1 egg
- 1/4 cup orange juice (smooth, not pulpy)
- 1 cup white flour
- 1 cup wheat flour (DO NOT substitute white flour!
- Various preserves, poppy seed or pie fillings (my favorite is apricot!)

Blend butter and sugar thoroughly. Add the egg and blend thoroughly. Add orange juice and blend thoroughly. Add flour, 1/2 cup at a time, alternating white and wheat, blending thoroughly between each. Refrigerate dough overnight or at least a few hours. Roll as thin as אַתָּה can without getting holes in the dough (roll it between two sheets of wax paper lightly dusted with flour for best results). Cut out 3 or 4 inch circles. Put a tablespoon of filling in the middle of each circle. Fold up the sides to make a triangle, overlapping the sides as much as possible so only a little filling shows through the middle. Squeeze the corners firmly, so they don't come undone while baking. Bake at 375 degrees for about 10-15 minutes, until golden brown but before the filling boils over!

Reading the מְגִילָה D7

Each _____, during פּוּרִים, the entire story of אֶסְתֵּר is read
year
aloud in a scroll called the מְגִילָה.

On the following pages, I have included my version of the מְגִילַת אֶסְתֵּר. To create your own מְגִילָה, print the three sheets (or go to hebrewwithjoy.com/hjbf-book-handouts/) on parchment-looking paper, tape the sheets together on the short ends and attach wooden dowels to each end. Use a ribbon to hold the scroll together.

Scroll of Esther מְגִלַּת אֶסְתֵּר

It all began in Ancient Persia in the 4th century BCE. The Holy Temple that had stood in Jerusalem was destroyed more than 50 years earlier, and the Jews were subjects of the mighty Persian empire which extended over 127 lands.

Three years after King Ahashuerus אֲחַשְׁוֵרוֹשׁ ascended the Persian throne, when he felt secure in his new position, he celebrated by throwing a grand 180-day-long party for all his subjects. Following this extravagant gala, Ahashuerus hosted a smaller week-long party for the residents of the capital city of Shushan (Susa) שׁוּשָׁן. In the palace's women's quarters, Ahashuerus' wife, Queen Vashti וַשְׁתִּי, hosted her own party for the Shushanite women.

On the seventh day of this party, Ahashuerus' heart "was merry with wine," and he commanded his wife Vashti to appear before all the partying men—he wanted to show them all her exquisite beauty. Vashti refused this request, then at the advice of his advisor Memuchan Ahashuerus ordered Vashti's banishment.

When Ahashuerus' wrath dissipated, he was lonely for a wife. His servants suggested that he orchestrate a beauty pageant. Officers would be appointed in all the king's lands, and all beautiful girls would be brought to Ahashuerus. And the girl who would find favor in the king's eyes would be the new queen.

There was a Jewish Shushanite resident named Mordechai מָרְדֳּכַי. He had a cousin, Hadassah הֲדַסָּה, who was orphaned as a young girl. Mordechai raised her and treated her as a daughter. Because she was beautiful, she was taken to the king's harem, to participate in the contest.

Her cousin Mordechai asked her to use the name Esther אֶסְתֵּר, to hide her Jewish identity. For a year, Esther and all the other contestants beautified themselves with perfumes and lotions. When Esther appeared before the king, he loved her more than any of the other women, and Esther became the new Queen of Persia. But as per Mordechai's directive, Esther refused to divulge her nationality—even to the king.

Shortly after Esther became queen, Mordechai overheard two of the king's chamberlains discussing a plot to assassinate the king. Mordechai had them reported, and the traitors were hanged.

Later, Haman הָמָן, one of Ahashuerus' ministers, was promoted to the position of Prime Minister. Haman was a violent Jew hater, in fact, he was a descendant of the notoriously anti-Semitic nation of Amalek.

Immediately after his promotion, the king issued a decree ordering everyone to bow down whenever Haman appeared. When Mordechai, a proud Jew, refused to bow down, Haman was infuriated.

He resolved to take revenge against all the Jews and threw lots ("purim" פּוּרִים) to determine the exact day when he would implement his plan. The lot ("pur") fell on the 13th day of the Hebrew month of Adar אֲדָר.

Haman approached Ahashuerus and offered him 10,000 silver talents in exchange for permission to exterminate the Jews. Ahashuerus told Haman, "The money is yours to keep, and the nation is yours to do with as you please."

1

99

Haman immediately sent proclamations to all the king's land. These declarations, sealed with the royal signet ring, ordered the people to rise up against the Jews and kill them all – men, women, and children – on the following 13th of Adar.

Mordechai became aware of the decree. He rent his garments and donned sackcloth. He sent a message to Esther, asking her to approach the king and beg him to spare her people. Esther responded that according to the rules anyone who entered the king's presence un-summoned would be put to death—unless the king extended to that person his golden scepter. "And I," Esther said, "have not been summoned by the king for thirty days already!"

Mordechai sent another message: "Do not think that you will escape the fate of all the Jews by being in the king's palace. For if you will remain silent at this time, relief and salvation will come to the Jews from another source, and you and the house of your father will be lost. And who knows if it is not for just such a time as this that you reached this royal position."

Esther agreed to approach the king. But she asked Mordechai to gather all the Jews in Shushan and ask them to fast for three days and nights. "After this, I will go to the king, even though it is against the law. So, if I perish, I perish."

Mordechai complied with Esther's request. He gathered all the Jews of Shushan and they fasted, repented and prayed to God. After three days of fasting, Esther donned royal garb and entered the king's chambers.

Immediately, he extended his scepter. "What is your request?" "I would like to invite the king and Haman to a small feast I have prepared," Esther responded.

So the king and Haman joined Esther for a feast. During the feast, the king again asked Esther whether she had anything to request. "Yes," Esther responded. "I would appreciate if tomorrow, again, the king and Haman would join me for a feast. And then I will tell the king my request."

Haman left the party a happy and proud man. Oh, the honor he was being accorded! But standing at the king's gate was Mordechai – who *still* refused to bow to Haman – and Haman was enraged. When he arrived home, his wife and wise advisors counseled him to erect a gallows, and then to go to the king and request permission to hang Mordechai. Haman excitedly went ahead and put up the gallows.

Sleep eluded the king that night, so he asked his servants to read to him from the Royal Chronicles. They complied with the king's orders. They read from the Chronicles how Mordechai saved the king's life when two of his chamberlains hatched a plot to kill him. "Was he rewarded for this fine act?" Ahashuerus asked. "No, he was not," the servants responded.

At that moment, Haman entered the king's courtyard. His purpose? To ask the king's permission to hang Mordechai! Before Haman could utter a word, Ahashuerus addressed him: "In your estimation, what shall be done to a person whom the king wishes to honor?"

2

Haman, who was certain that the king wished to honor him, responded: "Bring a royal garment and a royal horse. And let one of the king's nobles dress the man and lead him on the horse through the city streets, proclaiming before him, 'So is done for the man whom the king wishes to honor!'"

Ahashuerus responded: "Good! Now go get the garments and the horse and do so for Mordechai the Jew!" Haman had no choice but to comply. So, he went and honored Mordechai as the king had ordered.

Afterwards, he went home where his wife said, "Since Mordecai is Jewish, you won't be able to stand against him! In fact, you will certainly fall before him!" The king's men then took him to the banquet Esther had prepared.

"What is your request?" a curious King Ahashuerus asked Esther at the feast. "If I have found favor in your eyes, O King," Esther pleaded, "and if it pleases the king, let my life be granted me by my plea, and the life of my people by my request. For my people and I have been sold to be annihilated, killed and destroyed!"

Esther then identified Haman as the evil person who wished to perpetrate this atrocity. The king was greatly angered. When he was then informed that Haman had built gallows for Mordechai, he ordered that Haman be hanged on those very gallows. On that day, Haman's estate was given to Esther, and Mordechai was appointed Prime Minister in Haman's stead.

But Esther was far from satisfied. Haman was dead, but his evil decree was still in effect. According to Persian law, once a king issues a decree it cannot be rescinded. But the king gave Mordechai and Esther permission, and they promptly wrote up a decree that countermanded Haman's edict.

The decree granted the Jews permission to defend themselves against their enemies. On the 13th of Adar that year, the Jews throughout the Persian Empire mobilized and killed the enemies who had wanted to kill them. In Shushan, among the dead were Haman's ten sons.

Esther asked the king's permission for the Jews in Shushan to have one more day to destroy their enemy—and the king granted her wish. On that day, the 14th of Adar, the Jews worldwide celebrated, and the Jews of Shushan killed more of their enemies, and also hung Haman's sons. The Jews of Shushan then rested and celebrated on the 15th of Adar.

The Jews established a holiday to commemorate this amazing miracle of God. Jews worldwide celebrate on the 14th of Adar, while residents of walled cities — like Shushan — celebrate on the 15th of Adar. This holiday is called Purim, פּוּרִים for the word "pur" פּוּר (lot).

3

101

10 – Feast of Lots Exercises

שֵׁם _____

1. Read and translate the following עִבְרִית words.

שִׂמְחָה חֲנֻכָּה לַיְלָה פּוּרִים יְהוּדָה שָׁנָה יְהוּדִים מָרְדְּכַי קֹדֶשׁ
אֶסְתֵּר סֻכָּה מֶלֶךְ חֲנֻכִּיָּה יְשׁוּעָה יִשְׂרָאֵל תְּשׁוּבָה מְגִילָה שָׁבוּעוֹת

From this lesson, fill in the missing עִבְרִית and English words.

English	עִבְרִית	
	אֲחַשְׁוֵרוֹשׁ	.2
king		.3
	וַשְׁתִּי	.4
	מָרְדְּכַי	.5
Jews		.6
	הֲדַסָּה	.7
Esther		.8
	הָמָן	.9
lot		.10
	פּוּרִים	.11

12. Name 3 things that were hidden in the story of אֶסְתֵּר.

_____

_____

_____

13. _____Write the <u>root</u> meanings of ס.ת.ר.

14. Write one עִבְרִית word that comes from this root and the English meaning.

_____ E   _____ H

103

Post-Quiz

This post-quiz will show you how much you have learned about the vocabulary and roots of the מוֹעֲדִים. <u>Please don't use any resources to complete this page.</u>

2. Match the roots to their meaning.		
praise, give thanks _____	ר.א.שׁ	A
rule, reign _____	שׁ.ד.ח	B
cover, protect _____	שׁ.ל.ם	C
hide, conceal _____	ס.ת.ר	D
completion, wholeness _____	י.ד.ה	E
joyful, rejoice _____	שׂ.מ.ח	F
new, renew _____	שׁ.ב.ע	G
to return, turn back _____	א.מ.ן	H
truly _____	מ.ל.ך	I
seven _____	כ.פ.ר	J
head, beginning _____	שׁ.ו.ב	K

1. Match the words to their meaning.		
head _____	עִבְרִית	A
holiness _____	חַג	B
Hebrew _____	חֵטְא	C
repentance _____	מְלָאכָה	D
Jews _____	רֹאשׁ	E
sin _____	קָצִיר	F
holiday _____	יְהוּדִים	G
afflict, deny _____	עוֹלָם	H
harvest _____	קֹדֶשׁ	I
world/universe /forever _____	תְּשׁוּבָה	J
work _____	עָנָה	K

4. Match the holidays to their meaning.		
Day of the Atonements _____	חֲנֻכָּה	A
First Fruits _____	שַׁבָּת	B
Day of Blasting _____	יוֹם תְּרוּעָה	C
Feast of Weeks _____	הַמַּצוֹת	D
Feast of Dedication _____	פּוּרִים	E
Feast of Booths _____	פֶּסַח	F
Feast of Lots _____	בִּכּוּרִים	G
Sabbath _____	יוֹם הַכִּפֻּרִים	H
Unleavened Bread _____	סֻכּוֹת	I
Passover _____	שָׁבוּעוֹת	J

3. Match the words to their meaning.		
salvation _____	אוֹר	A
month _____	מֶלֶךְ	B
good _____	מוֹעֲדִים	C
year _____	יְשׁוּעָה	D
life _____	חֹדֶשׁ	E
king _____	צוֹם	F
light _____	שֶׁבַע	G
seven _____	חַיִּים	H
days _____	שָׁנָה	I
fast _____	טוֹב	J
appointed times _____	יָמִים	K

Answers are on the bottom of Appendix A

Continuing with Hebrew!

‏כָּל הַכָּבוֹד!‏ (all the כָּבוֹד!) for successfully completing *Hebrew with Joy! in the Biblical Feasts.* I pray it was an amazing experience studying Abba's Holy Language of עִבְרִית.

Please let me know if this book has blessed you and drawn you closer to our amazing LORD and His appointed times. <u>Would you take a moment to post a review on Amazon?</u>

If you have taken this course in a class setting, please complete the evaluation on the next page and give it to your teacher. Your מוֹרֶה or מוֹרָה will appreciate the feedback!

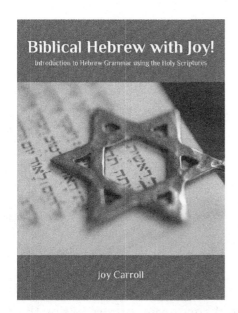

If your desire is to go deeper in your Biblical Hebrew understanding, study *Biblical Hebrew with Joy!: Introduction to Hebrew Grammar using the Holy Scriptures.* The book will help you to...

- Dig deep to learn the original intent of the writers
- Increase Biblical Hebrew vocabulary - 150 words!
- Learn key Hebrew roots and grammar
- Explore Israeli culture and rich traditions
- Read Hebrew Scriptures and prayers
- Study the Aaronic Blessing in Hebrew (see below)
- Use online Hebrew Bible tools
- Write personal Hebrew prayers
- Learn with Videos and Audios included!

יְבָרֶכְךָ יְהוָה וְיִשְׁמְרֶךָ׃

יָאֵר יְהוָה פָּנָיו אֵלֶיךָ וִיחֻנֶּךָּ׃

יִשָּׂא יְהוָה פָּנָיו אֵלֶיךָ וְיָשֵׂם לְךָ שָׁלוֹם׃

ADONAI will bless you and keep you!
ADONAI will make His face to shine on you and be gracious to you!
ADONAI will turn His face toward you and grant you *shalom*!

May you be blessed abundantly! My prayers are with you,
Your מוֹרָה (mo-RA) "teacher", Joy Carroll

Class Evaluation
Hebrew with Joy! in the Biblical Feasts

1. How would you rate this class on a scale of 1 to 5? (5 being the highest) _____

2. What did you like most about the class?

3. What suggestion/s do you have that would make the class better?

4. Would you be willing to write a book review that would encourage others to buy the book? Please post it through Amazon.com (search for: *Hebrew with Joy! in the Biblical Feasts*)

תּוֹדָה רַבָּה!

Appendix A
Hebrew Alphabet אָלֶף־בֵּית

Sound	Name	Script	Block	Letter
silent	**A**-lef			א
b as in **b**ar	Bet (with a dot)			בּ
v as in **v**ictory	Bet (without a dot)			ב
g as in **g**ap	**GEE**-mel			ג
d as in **d**oor	**DA**-let			ד
h as in **h**oly	Hay			ה
v as in **v**ictory	Vav			ו
z as in **z**eal	**ZAI**-yeen			ז
kh as in Ba**ch**	Khet			ח
t as in **t**op	Tet			ט
y as in **y**es	Yood			י
k as in **k**ing	Kaf (with a dot)			כּ
kh as in Ba**ch**	Kaf (without a dot)			כ
kh as in Ba**ch**	Kaf so-FEET			ך
l as in **l**ight	**LA**-med			ל
m as in **m**olehill	Mem			מ
m as in **m**olehill	Mem so-FEET			ם
n as in **n**ame	Noon			נ
n as in **n**ame	Noon so-FEET			ן

Hebrew Letters (cont.)

Sound	Name	Script	Block	Letter
s as in **s**on	**SA**-mekh	ס	ס	ס
silent	**AI**-yeen	ע	ע	ע
p as in **p**ray	Pay (with a dot)	פ	פ	פּ
f as in **f**aith	Pay (without a dot)	פ	פ	פ
f as in **f**aith	Pay so-FEET	ף	ף	ף
ts as in roo**ts**	**TSA**-dee	צ	צ	צ
ts as in roo**ts**	**TSA**-dee so-FEET	ץ	ץ	ץ
k as in **k**ing	Koof	ק	ק	ק
r as in **r**est	Raysh	ר	ר	ר
sh as in **sh**ine	Shin	ש	שׁ	שׁ
s as in **s**on	Shin	ש	שׂ	שׂ
t as in **t**oe	Tav	ת	ת	ת

Appendix B - Hebrew Vowels

Sounds like....	Nee-koo-dot - Vowels		
"a" as in <u>a</u>ll	ka-METZ	kha-TAF pa-TAKH	pa-TAKH
"o" as in <u>o</u>ver (dot is over the letter)	kho-LAM		kho-LAM ma-LE
"e" as in <u>e</u>gg (3+2=5 eggs in a basket)	se-GOL	kha-TAF se-GOL	TSE-ray
"ee" as in f<u>ee</u>t (the vowel is under the f<u>ee</u>t of the letter)	KHEE-reek ma-LE		KHEE-reek
silent or "uh" as in <u>a</u>bove (one dot above the other)	sh-VA		
"oo" as in t<u>oo</u> ("ooh- it hurts)	shoo-ROOK		koo-BOOTS
"akh" as in B<u>ach</u> (exception – at the end of a word)	khet with pa-TAKH		
"ay" as in l<u>ay</u> ("e" + "ee")	TSE-ray Yod		
"ai" as in p<u>ie</u> ("a" + "ee")	pa-TAKH yod		
"o" as in fl<u>ow</u> (exception vowel!)	kha-MATZ kha-TOOF		
"oy" as in t<u>oy</u>	kho-LAM ma-LE yod		
"ooey" as in g<u>ooey</u>	shoo-ROOK yod		

Appendix C – Flashcards

אֱלֹהִים	שַׁבָּת	שָׂמֵחַ
עִבְרִית	שׁ.ב.ת	חַג חַגִּים
קָדוֹשׁ	שׁ.ל.ם	קֹדֶשׁ
תּוֹרָה	שֵׁם	יִשְׂרָאֵל
יְהוָה	בָּרוּךְ	מוֹעֵד
שָׁלוֹם	מִקְרָא	מ.ל.ך

happy, rejoicing
ms 2

Sabbath
fs 1

GOD, god/s
ms, mpl   1

holiday/s, feast/s
ms, mpl 2

rest, stop
root 1

Hebrew
fs 1

holiness
mpl 2

completion, wholeness
root 1

holy
ms 1

Israel
fs 2

name
ms 1

instruction
fs 1

appointed time
ms 2

blessed
ms 2

LORD
ms 1

rule, reign
root 2

convocation
ms 2

peace, hello, goodbye
ms 1

מוֹעֲדִים	זָכוֹר	עוֹלָם
מֶלֶךְ	מְלָאכָה	יוֹם
יָמִים	בְּרָכָה	חָמֵץ
עֹנֶג	אָמֵן	חֹדֶשׁ
עֶרֶב	א.מ.ן	סֵדֶר
שָׁמוֹר	שַׁבָּת שָׁלוֹם	פֶּסַח

universe/world
forever
ms 3

remember
ms 3

appointed
times
mpl 2

day
ms 3

work
fs 3

king
ms 2

leaven
ms 4

blessing
fs 3

days
mpl 3

month
ms 4

so be it
3

delight
ms 3

order
ms 4

truly
root 3

evening
ms 3

Passover
ms 4

Sabbath of
Peace
phrase 3

observe,
guard, keep
ms 3

עֹמֶר	קָצִיר	אַתָּה
הַגָּדָה	רוּת	חַיִּים
מַצָּה מַצּוֹת	שֶׁבַע	שׁ.ב.ע
מָרוֹר	שִׁבְעָה	זִכָּרוֹן
ח.ד.שׁ	שָׁבוּעַ	תְּרוּעָה
בִּיכוּרִים	שָׁבוּעוֹת	טוֹב

Hebrew with Joy! in the Biblical Feasts

you ms 5	harvest ms 5	sheaf of grain ms 4
life ms 4	Ruth fs 5	the telling fs 4
seven root 5	seven fpl 5	unleavened bread/s fs fpl 4
remembrance ms 6	seven mpl 5	bitter herbs ms 4
blast, shout fs 6	week ms 5	new, renew root 4
good ms, fs 6	weeks mpl 5	first fruits mpl 5

רֹאשׁ	ר.א.שׁ	נֶפֶשׁ
לֹא	עָנָה	אֱלֹהֵיכֶם
שׁוֹפָר	כִּפֵּר	שׁ.ו.ב
שָׁנָה	טָהוֹר	כ.פ.ר
תְּשׁוּבָה	צוֹם	חָטָא
אֶתְרוֹג	אֵשׁ	סֻכָּה סֻכּוֹת

soul

fs 7

head, beginning,
chief, top

root 6

head

ms 6

אֱלֹהֶיךָyour

ms 7

afflict, deny

ms 7

no, not

6

to return,
turn back

root 7

atone,
atonement

ms 7

ram's
horn

ms 6

cover,
protect

root 7

clean, purified

ms 7

year

fs 6

sin

ms 7

fast

ms 7

repentance

fs 7

booth/s
tabernacle/s

fs fpl 8

fire

fs 7

citron

ms 8

לוּלָב	זְמַן שִׂמְחַתֵנוּ	אוֹר
פְּרִי	שׂ.מ.ח	נֵס
שִׂמְחָה	מְנוֹרָה	לַיְלָה
שִׂמְחַת	חֲנֻכִּיָּה	שֶׁמֶן
בְּנֵי	חֲנֻכָּה	יְשׁוּעָה
שֶׁמֶשׁ	יְהוּדָה	י.ד.ה

light
ms 9

season/time of
our joy
phrase 8

date palm
branch
ms 8

miracle
ms 9

joyful,
rejoice,
be glad
root 8

fruit
ms 8

night
ms 9

7-branched
lamp stand
fs 9

joy
fs 8

oil
ms 9

9-branched
lamp stand
fs 9

joy of..
fs 8

salvation
fs 9

dedication
fs 9

sons/children
of..
mpl 8

praise, give
thanks
root 9

Judah
ms 9

caretaker
ms 9

חַג חֲנֻכָּה שָׂמֵחַ	חַג פּוּרִים שָׂמֵחַ	מְגִילָה
אֲחַשְׁוֵרוֹשׁ	פּוּר	
אֶסְתֵּר	פּוּרִים	
הֲדַסָּה	מָרְדְּכַי	
הָמָן	וַשְׁתִּי	
יְהוּדִים	ס.ת.ר	

scroll
fs 10

Happy Feast of
Lots holiday
10

Happy Feast of
Dedication
holiday   9

lot
ms 10

Ahasuerus
ms 10

lots
mpl 10

Esther
fs 10

Mordecai
ms 10

Hadassah
fs 10

Vashti
fs 10

Haman
ms 10

hide, conceal
root 10

Jews
mpl 10

Appendix D - Lesson Fill-Ins

Fill-Ins from right to left!	Line/s	Lesson
תּוֹרָה, יְהֹוָה	C8	1
שָׁלוֹם, Sabbath	D4, D7	1
קָדוֹשׁ, holidays/feasts	A11	2
(of) convocation, LORD, appointed times appointed times, holiness	B4	2
Passover, Feast of Lots, Feast of Booths, Sabbath Feast of Weeks	C2	2
Day of the Atonements, Day of Blasting Feast of Dedication, Feast of Unleavened Bread	C3	2
מֶלֶךְ	E1	2
Happy Feast of Booths Holiday Happy Passover Holiday Happy Feast of Dedication Holiday	G3	2
חַג שָׁבוּעוֹת שָׂמֵחַ!	G4	2
יְהֹוָה	I1	2
שַׁבָּת, יְהֹוָה	B6	3
זָכוֹר, יוֹם, Sabbath	B8	3
שָׁמוֹר, יוֹם, הַשַּׁבָּת, לְקַדְּשׁוֹ	B10	3
to/for Israel, the days, to holy it, the evening, the blessing	C3	3
delight	E1	3
so be it, the universe, the, מֶלֶךְ, our GOD, יְהֹוָה, you, בָּרוּךְ	E2	3
אָמֵן	G2	3
יְהֹוָה, יוֹם, הַשַּׁבָּת, זָכוֹר, שָׁמוֹר, לְקַדְּשׁוֹ, עֹנֶג, אָמֵן	H	3
observe/guard/keep, חֹדֶשׁ, the spring, פֶּסַח, to/for LORD, אֱלֹהִים	B2	4
חֹדֶשׁ	C	4
מִצְוֹת	D2	4
יוֹם	E2	4
F-the tellings, M-months, F-unleavened breads, M-days	G4	4
חָמֵץ, order	H1, H4	4
אֱלֹהִים, lovingkindness	H5, I2	4
holiday/feast of the harvest, בִּיכּוּרִים	B1-B2	5
קָצִיר, רוּת	B5-B6	5
תּוֹרָה	C3	5
so be it, the instruction, יְהֹוָה, you, בָּרוּךְ	D4	5

Fill-Ins from right to left!	Line/s	Lesson
LORD, blessing, days, blessings, months, Sabbaths	E3	5
M-four days, M-six months, F-two Sabbaths M-one harvest, F-one blessing, F-seven blessings	E4	5
weeks ,שָׁבוּעַ, seven	F1	5
יְהוָה, אַתָּה, שָׁבוּעוֹת, בִּיכוּרִים, קָצִיר, אַתָּה, תּוֹרָה, אַתָּה, יוֹם, אָמֵן	H	5
blasting, יוֹם, לֹא work, to/for, holiness, convocation	B4-B6	6
רֹאשׁ	C1	6
חֹדֶשׁ שִׁשִּׁי, שְׁבִיעִי, תִּשְׁרֵי	D3	6
שׁוֹפָר, רֹאשׁ	E3, E5	6
מְלָאכָה	F5	6
your (mpl) souls, your (mpl) GOD , foreigner, native-born	C2, C4	7
נֶפֶשׁ, מְלָאכָה, צוֹם	D1-D3	7
כִּפֻּר, Day of the Atonements, תְּשׁוּבָה	E1-E2	7
צוֹם	F10	7
תּוֹרָה, יְהוָה	G2-G3	7
חַג הַסֻּכּוֹת, סֻכּוֹת, יָמִים	B1, B5	8
קָצִיר	C1	8
שִׂמְחָה, joy of, שָׂמֵחַ	D	8
שָׂמֵחַ, יִשְׂרָאֵל, פְּרִי, joy	E1-E2, E7-E8	8
Joy of instruction, אֱלֹהִים of Israel, Day of the Atonements Sabbath of Peace, sons/children of Israel	F5-F9	8
שִׂמְחָה, יְהוָה	H1-I1	8
the universe, king, our אֱלֹהִים, LORD, You, blessed	J3	8
חֹדֶשׁ, dedication	B3, B5	9
They were remembering סֻכּוֹת which they had missed.	B7	9
יְהוּדָה	C	9
שֶׁמֶן, חֲנֻכִּיָּה	D1	9
my instruction, my soul, salvation, and, light, יְהוָה, Psalms	E1, E4	9
חֲנֻכָּה, חַג, תּוֹרָה	F2, F3, F5	9
מֶלֶךְ, חֹדֶשׁ	B3, B5	10
אֶסְתֵּר, יְהוּדִים	B9, B11	10
אֶסְתֵּר, יְהוּדִים	C1, C2	10
פּוּרִים, שָׁנָה	D1, D7	10

Appendix E - Roots

Lesson	Meaning	Root
1	rest, stop	שׁ.ב.ת
1	completion, wholeness	שׁ.ל.ם
2	rule, reign	מ.ל.ך
3	truly	א.מ.ן
4	new, renew	ח.ד.שׁ
5	seven	שׁ.ב.ע
6	head, beginning	ר.א.שׁ
7	cover, protect	כ.פ.ר
7	to return, turn back	שׁ.ו.ב
8	joyful, rejoice	שׂ.מ.ח
9	praise, give thanks	י.ד.ה
10	hide, conceal	ס.ת.ר

Appendix F - Holiday Phrases

Holiday	English	Transliteration	Hebrew
All	Happy Holiday!	khag sa-**ME**-akh!	חַג שָׂמֵחַ!
Sabbath	Peaceful Sabbath!	sha-BAT sha-LOM	שַׁבָּת שָׁלוֹם!
Passover	Happy Passover holiday!	khag **PE**-sakh sa-**ME**-akh!	חַג פֶּסַח שָׂמֵחַ!
Feast of Weeks	Happy Feast of Weeks holiday!	khag sha-voo-OT sa-**ME**-akh!	חַג שָׁבוּעוֹת שָׂמֵחַ!
Day of Blasting	Happy Day of Blasting holiday!	khag yom t-roo-A sa-**ME**-akh!	חַג יוֹם תְּרוּעָה שָׂמֵחַ!
(Traditional) Rosh Hashanah	To a good and sweet year!	la-sha-NA to-VA oo-me-too-KA	לְשָׁנָה טוֹבָה וּמְתוּקָה!
Day of the Atonements	(May you) finish inscribed for good	ga-MAR kha-tee-MA to-VA	גְּמַר חֲתִימָה טוֹבָה.
Feast of Booths	Season of our Joy	z-MAN seem-kha-**TE**-noo	זְמַן שִׂמְחָתֵנוּ
Feast of Dedication	Happy Feast of Dedication holiday!	khag kha-noo-KA sa-**ME**-akh!	חַג חֲנֻכָּה שָׂמֵחַ!
Feast of Lots	Happy Feast of Lots holiday!	khag poo-REEM sa-**ME**-akh!	חַג פּוּרִים שָׂמֵחַ!

Appendix G - Resources

Ancient Hebrew Research Center
Ancient Hebrew Dictionary
Jeff A. Benner
Ancient-hebrew.org

Celebrate the Feasts
Martha Zimmerman
Bethany House publishers c. 1981

The Festivals
First Fruits of Zion
https://ffoz.org/

Torah Resource
Tim Hegg
https://torahresource.com/the-yearly-festivals

Torah Class
Tom Bradford
www.torahclass.com

Voice for Israel
Hannah Nesher
https://www.voiceforisrael.net/festival-readings
Nesher.hannah@gmail.com

Worthy Ministries
George Whitten
https://worthybrief.com

Wikipedia
https://en.wikipedia.org/

Appendix H – Hebrew Months

Time of Year	Number of Days	Post-exile English Transliteration	Post-exile Hebrew Name	Biblical English Name	Biblical Hebrew Name	Month # in Bible
Mar-Apr	30	Nisan (nee-SAN)	נִיסָן Neh. 2:1 Esther 3:7	Aviv Exodus 13:4, 23:15, 34:18, Deut. 16:1 1st month	אָבִיב חֹדֶשׁ רִאשׁוֹן	1
Apr-May	29	Iyar (ee-YAR)	אִיָּיר	Ziv 1 Kings 6:1 2nd month	זִו חֹדֶשׁ שֵׁנִי	2
May–Jun	30	Sivan (see-VAN)	סִיוָן	3rd month	חֹדֶשׁ שְׁלִישִׁי	3
Jun-Jul	29	Tammuz (ta-MOOZ)	תַּמּוּז	4th month	חֹדֶשׁ רְבִיעִי	4
Jul-Aug	30	Av (av)	אָב	5th month	חֹדֶשׁ חֲמִישִׁי	5
Aug-Sept	29	Elul (eh-LOOL)	אֱלוּל	6th month	חֹדֶשׁ שִׁשִּׁי	6
Sept-Oct	30	Tishrei (teesh-RAY)	תִּשְׁרִי	Etanim 1 Kings 8:2 7th month	אֵתָנִים חֹדֶשׁ שְׁבִיעִי	7
Oct-Nov	29 or 30	Cheshvan (khesh-VAN)	חֶשְׁוָן	Bul 1 Kings 6:38 8th month	בּוּל חֹדֶשׁ שְׁמִינִי	8
Nov-Dec	30 or 29	Kislev (kees-LEV)	כִּסְלֵו	9th month	חֹדֶשׁ תְּשִׁיעִי	9
Dec-Jan	29	Tevet (TE-vet)	טֵבֵת	10th month	חֹדֶשׁ עֲשִׂירִי	10
Jan-Feb	30	Shevat (sh-VAT)	שְׁבָט	11th month	עַשְׁתֵּי־עָשָׂר חֹדֶשׁ	11
Feb-Mar	29	Adar* (a-DAR)	אֲדָר	12th month	שְׁנֵי־עָשָׂר חֹדֶשׁ	12

*Periodically, an extra month of Adar (called Adar Bet) is added to the Jewish Calendar.

Appendix l – Hebrew Days of the Week

Day starts from sundown	Day continues until sundown	English Translation	Day of the week (English)	Day of the week (Hebrew)
Saturday	Sunday	first day	yom ree-SHON	יוֹם רִאשׁוֹן
Sunday	Monday	second day	yom she-NEE	יוֹם שֵׁנִי
Monday	Tuesday	third day	yom sh-lee-SHEE	יוֹם שְׁלִישִׁי
Tuesday	Wednesday	fourth day	yom r-vee-EE	יוֹם רְבִיעִי
Wednesday	Thursday	fifth day	yom kha-mee-SHEE	יוֹם חֲמִישִׁי
Thursday	Friday	sixth day	yom shee-SHEE	יוֹם שִׁשִׁי
Friday	Saturday	Shabbat (Sabbath)	sha-BAT	שַׁבָּת

Appendix J1 – Hebrew Cardinal Numbers

Feminine (i.e. time, counting)		Masculine (i.e. money)		Number
a-KHAT	אַחַת	e-KHAD	אֶחָד	1
sh-**TA**-yeem	שְׁתַּיִם	sh-**NA**-yeem	שְׁנַיִם	2
sha-LOSH	שָׁלוֹשׁ	sh-lo-SHA	שְׁלוֹשָׁה	3
ar-BA	אַרְבַּע	ar-ba-A	אַרְבָּעָה	4
kha-MESH	חָמֵשׁ	kha-mee-SHA	חֲמִשָּׁה	5
shesh	שֵׁשׁ	shee-SHA	שִׁשָּׁה	6
SHE-va	שֶׁבַע	sheev-A	שִׁבְעָה	7
sh-mo-NE	שְׁמוֹנֶה	sh-mo-NA	שְׁמוֹנָה	8
TE-sha	תֵּשַׁע	teesh-A	תִּשְׁעָה	9
E-ser	עֶשֶׂר	a-sa-RA	עֲשָׂרָה	10
a-KHAT es-RE	אַחַת עֶשְׂרֵה	a-KHAD a-SAR	אַחַד עָשָׂר	11
sh-TAYM es-RE	שְׁתֵּים עֶשְׂרֵה	sh-NAYM a-SAR	שְׁנֵים עָשָׂר	12
sha-LOSH es-RE	שְׁלוֹשׁ עֶשְׂרֵה	sh-lo-SHA a-SAR	שְׁלוֹשָׁה עָשָׂר	13
ar-BA es-RE	אַרְבַּע עֶשְׂרֵה	ar-ba-A a-SAR	אַרְבָּעָה עָשָׂר	14
kha-MESH es-RE	חֲמֵשׁ עֶשְׂרֵה	kha-mee-SHA a-SAR	חֲמִשָּׁה עָשָׂר	15
es-REEM עֶשְׂרִים				20
es-REEM v-a-KHAT	עֶשְׂרִים וְאַחַת	es-REEM v-a-KHAD	עֶשְׂרִים וְאֶחָד	21
kha-mee-SHEEM חֲמִישִׁים				50

Appendix J2 – Hebrew Ordinal Numbers

Hebrew Feminine	Hebrew Masculine	English
רִאשׁוֹנָה (ree-sho-NA)	רִאשׁוֹן (ree-SHON)	first
שְׁנִיָּה (sh-nee-YA)	שֵׁנִי (she-NEE)	second
שְׁלִישִׁית (sh-lee-SHEET)	שְׁלִישִׁי (sh-lee-SHEE)	third
רְבִיעִית (r-vee-EET)	רְבִיעִי (r-vee-EE)	fourth
חֲמִישִׁית (kha-mee-SHEET)	חֲמִישִׁי (kha-mee-SHEE)	fifth
שִׁשִּׁית (shee-SHEET)	שִׁשִּׁי (shee-SHEE)	sixth
שְׁבִיעִית (sh-vee-EET)	שְׁבִיעִי (sh-vee-EE)	seventh
שְׁמִינִית (sh-mee-EET)	שְׁמִינִי (sh-mee-NEE)	eighth
תְּשִׁיעִית (t-shee-EET)	תְּשִׁיעִי (t-shee-EE)	ninth
עֲשִׂירִית (a-see-REET)	עֲשִׂירִי (a-see-REE)	tenth

Note: For ordinal numbers greater than 10, cardinal numbers are used instead.

Appendix K – Tanakh Book Names

English Name	Hebrew	Transliteration
1st Chronicles	דִּבְרֵי הַיָּמִים א	deev-RAY ha-ya-MEEM A-lef
2nd Chronicles	דִּבְרֵי הַיָּמִים ב	deev-RAY ha-ya-MEEM bet
Amos	עָמוֹס	a-MOS
Daniel	דָּנִיֵּאל	da-nee-YEL
Deuteronomy	דְּבָרִים	d-va-REEM
Ecclesiastes	קֹהֶלֶת	ko-**HE**-let
Esther	אֶסְתֵּר	es-TER
Exodus	שְׁמוֹת	sh-MOT
Ezekiel	יְחֶזְקֵאל	y-khez-KEL
Ezra	עֶזְרָא	ez-RA
Genesis	בְּרֵאשִׁית	b-re-SHEET
Habakkuk	חֲבַקּוּק	kha-va-KOOK
Haggai	חַגַּי	kha-GAI
Hosea	הוֹשֵׁעַ	ho-**SHAY**-a
Isaiah	יְשַׁעְיָהוּ	y-sha-**YA**-hoo
Jeremiah	יִרְמְיָהוּ	yeer-m-**YA**-hoo
Job	אִיּוֹב	ee-OV
Joel	יוֹאֵל	yo-EL
Jonah	יוֹנָה	yo-NA
Joshua	יְהוֹשֻׁעַ	y-**HO**-shoo-a
Judges	שׁוֹפְטִים	shof-TEEM
Kings	מְלָכִים	m-la-KHEEM
Lamentations	אֵיכָה	ay-KHA
Leviticus	וַיִּקְרָא	va-yeek-RA
Malachi	מַלְאָכִי	mal-a-KHEE
Micah	מִיכָה	mee-KHA

Appendix K – Tanakh Book Names 2

English Name	Hebrew	Transliteration
Nahum	נַחוּם	na-KHUM
Nehemiah	נְחֶמְיָה	n-khem-YA
Numbers	בַּמִּדְבָּר	ba-meed-BAR
Obadiah	עֹבַדְיָה	o-vad-YA
Proverbs	מִשְׁלֵי	meesh-LAY
Psalms	תְּהִלִּים	t-hee-LEEM
Ruth	רוּת	root
Samuel	שְׁמוּאֵל	shmoo-EL
Song of Songs	שִׁיר הַשִּׁירִים	sheer ha-shee-REEM
Zechariah	זְכַרְיָה	z-khar-YA
Zephaniah	צְפַנְיָה	ts-fan-YA

Appendix L - Dictionary

Lesson	English	Gender	Transliteration	Hebrew
1	Abraham	ms	av-ra-HAM	אַבְרָהָם
7	afflict/deny	ms	a-NA	עָנָה
7	again		shoov	שׁוּב
10	Ahasuerus	ms	a-khash-ve-ROSH	אֲחַשְׁוֵרוֹשׁ
10	all		kol	כָּל
10	all the glory (honor)		kol ha-ka-VOD	כָּל הַכָּבוֹד
7	all vows	mpl	kol need-RAY	כָּל נִדְרֵי
2	appointed time (festival, season, feast)	ms	mo-ED	מוֹעֵד
2	appointed times	mpl	mo-a-DEEM	מוֹעֲדִים
8	assembly	ms	a-**TSE**-ret	עֲצֶרֶת
7	atone, atonement	ms	kee-POOR	כִּפֻּר
7	atonement cover	fs	ka-**PO**-ret	כַּפֹּרֶת
3	believe		ma-a-MEEN	מַאֲמִין
6	binding	fs	a-kee-DA	עֲקֵידָה
4	bitter herbs	ms	ma-ROR	מָרוֹר
6	blast/shout	fs	t-roo-A	תְּרוּעָה
2	blessed	ms	ba-ROOKH	בָּרוּךְ
3	blessing	fs	b-ra-KHA	בְּרָכָה
8	booth, tabernacle	fs	soo-KA	סֻכָּה
8	booths, tabernacles	fpl	soo-KOT	סֻכּוֹת
9	7-branched lamp stand	fs	m-no-RA	מְנוֹרָה
9	9-branched lamp stand	fs	kha-noo-**KEE**-ya	חֲנֻכִּיָּה
9	caretaker	ms	sha-MASH	שַׁמָּשׁ
8	citron (large yellow fruit similar to a lemon)	ms	et-ROG	אֶתְרוֹג
7	clean/pure	ms	ta-HOR	טָהוֹר
2	convocation	ms	meek-RA	מִקְרָא
3	creator	ms	bo-RE	בּוֹרֵא
8	date palm branch	ms	loo-LAV	לוּלָב
3	day	ms	yom (ms)	יוֹם
3	days	mpl	ya-MEEM (mpl)	יָמִים
6	Days of Awe	mpl	ya-MEEM no-ra-EEM	יָמִים נוֹרָאִים
9	dedication	fs	kha-noo-KA	חֲנֻכָּה
3	delight	ms	**O**-neg	עֹנֶג
5	desert	ms	*meed-BAR*	מִדְבָּר
7	dome (skullcap)	fs	kee-PA	כִּיפָּה

Lesson	English	Gender	Transliteration	Hebrew
8	dwell, sit	ms	ya-SHAV	יָשַׁב
8	eighth	ms	sh-mee-NEE	שְׁמִינִי
10	Esther	fs	es-TER	אֶסְתֵּר
3	evening	ms	**E**-rev	עֶרֶב
3	faith	fs	e-moo-NA	אֱמוּנָה
7	fast (abstain from something)	ms	tsom	צוֹם
9	Feast of Lights	ms	khag ha-oo-REEM	חַג הָאוּרִים
8	Feast of the Ingathering	ms	khag ha-a-SEEF	חַג הָאָסִיף
7	fire	fs	esh	אֵשׁ
6	first	ms	ree-SHON	רִאשׁוֹן
5	first fruits	mpl	bee-koo-REEM	בִּיכּוּרִים
6	First Hebrew month - post exile	ms	nee-SAN	נִיסָן
6	first month	ms	KHO-desh ree-SHON	חֹדֶשׁ רִאשׁוֹן
6	fish	ms	dag	דָּג
5	five (f)	f	kha-MESH	חָמֵשׁ
5	five (m)	m	kha-mee-SHA	חֲמִשָּׁה
5	flower wreath	ms	zer p-ra-KHEEM	זֵר פְּרָחִים
5	four (f)	f	ar-BA	אַרְבַּע
5	four (m)	m	ar-ba-A	אַרְבָּעָה
8	fruit	ms	p-REE	פְּרִי
1	אֱלֹהִים , אֱלֹהִים	ms/mpl	e-lo-HEEM	אֱלֹהִים
3	going up by foot	fs	a-lee-YA l-**RE**-gel	עֲלִייָה לְרֶגֶל
6	good (fem)	fs	to-VA	טוֹבָה
6	good (masc)	ms	tov	טוֹב
10	Hadassah	fs	ha-da-SA	הֲדַסָּה
10	Haman	ms	ha-MAN	הָמָן
10	Haman's ears	mpl	oz-NAY ha-MAN	אָזְנֵי־הָמָן
9	hand	ms	yad	יָד
2, 8	happy, rejoicing	ms	sa-**ME**-akh	שָׂמֵחַ
5	harvest	ms	ka-TSEER	קָצִיר
6	head	ms	rosh	רֹאשׁ
6	head of the year	ms	rosh ha-sha-NA	רֹאשׁ הַשָּׁנָה
3	hear/listen	ms	sh-MA	שְׁמַע
1	Hebrew	fs	eev-REET	עברית
10	hidden		e-sa-TER	אֶסְתֵּר
10	hide		as-TEER	אַסְתִּיר
2	holiday, feast	ms	khag	חַג

135

Lesson	English	Gender	Transliteration	Hebrew
2	holidays, feasts	mpl	kha-GEEM	חַגִּים
2	holiness	ms	**KO**-desh	קֹדֶשׁ
1	holy	ms	ka-DOSH	קָדוֹשׁ
3	Immanuel	ms	ee-**MA**-noo el	עִמָּנוּ אֵל
4	in order	ms	b-**SE**-der	בְּסֵדֶר
1	instruction (1st 5 books of Bible)	fs	to-RA	תּוֹרָה
1	Isaac	ms	yeets-KHAK	יִצְחָק
2	Israel	fs	yees-ra-EL	יִשְׂרָאֵל
1	Jacob	ms	ya-a-KOV	יַעֲקֹב
1	Jerusalem	fs	y-roo-sha-**LAI**-yeem	יְרוּשָׁלַיִם
9	Jew, Jewish	ms	y-hoo-DEE	יְהוּדִי
10	Jews	mpl	y-hoo-DEEM	יְהוּדִים
8	Joy (noun)	fs	seem-KHA	שִׂמְחָה
8	joy of...	fs	*seem-KHAT*	שִׂמְחַת
9	Judah	ms	y-hoo-DA	יְהוּדָה
10	king	ms	**ME**-lekh	מֶלֶךְ
2	kingdom	fs	mal-KHOOT	מַלְכוּת
4	leaven	ms	kha-METS	חָמֵץ
4	life	ms	kha-YEEM	חַיִּים
9	light	ms	or	אוֹר
4	live	ms	khai	חַי
1	LORD	ms	a-do-NAI	יְהוָה
10	lot (to cast)	ms	poor	פּוּר
10	lots	mpl	poo-REEM	פּוּרִים
4	loving-kindness, mercy	ms	**KHE**-sed	חֶסֶד
9	Maccabee	ms	ma-ka-BEE	מַכַּבִּי
6	Memorial Day	ms	yom ha-zee-ka-RON	יוֹם הַזִּכָּרוֹן
9	miracle	ms	nes	נֵס
4	month	ms	**KHO**-desh	חֹדֶשׁ
4	months	mpl	kho-da-SHEEM	חֳדָשִׁים
10	Mordecai	ms	mor-do-KHAI	מָרְדְּכַי
1	Moses	ms	mo-SHE	מֹשֶׁה
1	name	ms	shem	שֵׁם
4	new	ms	kha-DASH	חָדָשׁ
4	new covenant	fs	breet kha-da-SHA	בְּרִית חֲדָשָׁה
3	new moon	ms	rosh **KHO**-desh	רֹאשׁ חֹדֶשׁ
9	night	ms	**LAI**-la	לַיְלָה

Lesson	English	Gender	Transliteration	Hebrew
6	no, not	-	*lo*	לֹא
5	oath	*fs*	*sh-voo-A*	שְׁבוּעָה
3	observe, guard, keep	*ms*	*sha-MOR*	שָׁמוֹר
9	oil	*ms*	**SHE**-*men*	שֶׁמֶן
5	one (f)	*f*	*a-KHAT*	אַחַת
5	one (m)	*m*	*e-KHAD*	אֶחָד
4	order (Passover service)	*ms*	**SE**-*der*	סֵדֶר
4	Passover	*ms*	**PE**-*sakh*	פֶּסַח
1	peace, hello, goodbye	*ms*	*sha-LOM*	שָׁלוֹם
1	perfection	*fs*	*shle-MOOT*	שְׁלֵמוּת
4	praise	*ms*	*ha-LEL*	הַלֵּל
2	queen	*fs*	*mal-KA*	מַלְכָּה
6	ram's horn	*ms*	*sho-FAR*	שׁוֹפָר
3	remember	*ms*	*za-KHOR*	זָכוֹר
6	remembrance	*ms*	*zee-ka-RON*	זִכָּרוֹן
7	repentance	*fs*	*t-shoo-VA*	תְּשׁוּבָה
5	Ruth	*fs*	*root*	רוּת
1	Sabbath	*fs*	*sha-BAT*	שַׁבָּת
1	Sabbaths	*fpl*	*sha-ba-TOT*	שַׁבָּתוֹת
1	Sabbatical	*fs*	*sha-ba-TON*	שַׁבָּתוֹן
4	sacrifice	*ms*	*kor-BAN*	קָרְבָּן
9	salvation	*fs*	*y-shoo-AH*	יְשׁוּעָה
3	sanctification	*ms*	*kee-DOOSH*	קִדּוּשׁ
10	scroll	*fs*	*m-gee-LA*	מְגִילָה
10	scroll of Esther	*fs*	*m-gee-LAT es-TER*	מְגִילַת אֶסְתֵּר
8	Season of our Joy	*ms*	*z-MAN seem-kha-**TAY**-noo*	זְמַן שִׂמְחָתֵנוּ
3	separation	*fs*	*hav-da-LA*	הַבְדָּלָה
5	seven (fem)	*fpl*	**SHE**-*va*	שֶׁבַע
5	seven (masc)	*mpl*	*sheev-A*	שִׁבְעָה
5	seventh (f)	*f*	*sh-vee-EET*	שְׁבִיעִית
5	seventh (m)	*m*	*sh-vee-EE*	שְׁבִיעִי
6	seventh month -post exile	*mpl*	*teesh-RAY*	תִּשְׁרֵי
4	sheaf (of grain)	*ms*	**O**-*mer*	עֹמֶר
7	sin	*ms*	*khet*	חֵטְא
3	so be it	-	*a-MEN*	אָמֵן
1	Solomon	*ms*	*shlo-MO*	שְׁלֹמֹה
8	sons of...	*mpl*	*b-NAY*	בְּנֵי

Lesson	English	Gen	Transliteration	Hebrew
7	soul	fs	**NE**-fesh	נֶפֶשׁ
5	speak/talk	ms	m-da-BER	מְדַבֵּר
9	spinning top	ms	s-vee-VON	סְבִיבוֹן
4	spring, first month	ms	a-VEEV	אָבִיב
6	Sunday	ms	yom ree-SHON	יוֹם רִאשׁוֹן
10	teacher	ms	mo-RE	מוֹרֶה
10	teacher	fs	mo-RA	מוֹרָה
6	Ten days of Repentance	mpl	a-sa-RA ya-MAY t-shoo-VA	עֲשָׂרָה יְמֵי תְּשׁוּבָה
9	thanks		to-DA	תּוֹדָה
4	the telling (Passover book)	fs	ha-ga-DA	הַגָּדָה
5	three (f)	f	sha-LOSH	שָׁלוֹשׁ
5	three (m)	m	sh-lo-SHA	שְׁלוֹשָׁה
3	three legs	mpl	sha-LOSH rag-**LAI**-yeem	שָׁלוֹשׁ רְגָלַיִם
2	to reign		leem-LOKH	לִמְלוֹךְ
1	to rest		leesh-BOT	לִשְׁבּוֹת
7	to return		la-SHOOV	לָשׁוּב
1	to sit		la-**SHE**-vet	לָשֶׁבֶת
7	to/for you	mpl	la-KHEM	לָכֶם
9	train (up)	ms	kha-NOKH	חֲנֹךְ
3	truth	fs	**E**-met	אֱמֶת
5	two (f)	f	sh-**TA**-yeem	שְׁתַּיִם
5	two (m)	m	sh-**NA**-yeem	שְׁנַיִם
3	universe/world/forever	ms	o-LAM	עוֹלָם
4	unleavened bread	fs	ma-TSA	מַצָּה
4	unleavened breads	fpl	ma-TSOT	מַצּוֹת
10	Vashti	fs	vash-TEE	וַשְׁתִּי
5	week	ms	sha-**VOO**-a	שָׁבוּעַ
5	weeks	mpl	sha-voo-OT	שָׁבוּעוֹת
5	Western Wall	ms	ha-ma-a-ra-VEE ha-ko-TEL	הַמַּעֲרָבִי הַכּוֹתֶל
3	who brings forth	ms	ha-**MO**-tsee	הַמּוֹצִיא
3	who has kept us alive	ms	she-he-khe-**YA**-noo	שֶׁהֶחֱיָנוּ
1	whole, complete	ms	sha-LEM	שָׁלֵם
8	word pairs	fpl	s-mee-KHOOT	סְמִיכוּת
3	work (occupation/employment)	fs	m-la-KHA	מְלָאכָה
6	year	fs	sha-NA	שָׁנָה
5	you	ms	a-TA	אַתָּה
6	you will throw	ms	tash-LEEKH	תַּשְׁלִיךְ

Appendix M Feast Summary

שָׁמוֹר	זָכוֹר	מוֹעֵד
Honor and keep the 7th יוֹם of שַׁבָּת, Fellowship with others in a מִקְרָא־קֹדֶשׁ. שַׁבָּת is a 24-hour יוֹם starting on Friday עֶרֶב where we delight in אֱלֹהִים and His works.	Gen. 2:1-3, Ex. 20:8-11, 31:13,16 Lev. 23:3, Deut. 5:15, Is. 56:2, Is. 58:13-14 שַׁבָּת is a memorial of the 7th יוֹם of creation when יְהֹוָה rested from His work, blessed the 7th יוֹם, and made it קָדוֹשׁ.	שַׁבָּת Sabbath Every 7th day (Friday at sundown-until Saturday at sundown)
יְהֹוָה commands us to celebrate פֶּסַח every year. For 7 יָמִים, eat מַצָּה (bread without חָמֵץ). On the first and last יוֹם, have a מִקְרָא־קֹדֶשׁ with no מְלָאכָה. The יוֹם after the שַׁבָּת of the חַג, begin to count the עֹמֶר. Traditionally, עֶרֶב פֶּסַח starts with a special meal called a סֵדֶר which is guided by a book called a הַגָּדָה.	Ex. 12, 34:18, Lev. 23:5-10, Deut. 16:1-8 פֶּסַח is a remembrance of freedom from the slavery of Egypt. The lamb was slain, and the blood was applied to the doorposts so that the angel of death would pass over the עִבְרִית homes. Then, the people left Egypt in haste to cross the Red Sea on the way to the Promised land. פֶּסַח also celebrates the first fruits of the barley harvest that is waved before יְהֹוָה.	פֶּסַח Passover 14th day of 1st mo. Aviv (Nisan) חַג הַמַּצּוֹת Unleavened Bread 15-22 day of 1st mo. Aviv (Nisan) עֹמֶר Waving of the Omer Day after Sabbath during Passover March-April
Celebrate שָׁבוּעוֹת 50 days after the שַׁבָּת of פֶּסַח, have a מִקְרָא־קֹדֶשׁ with no מְלָאכָה. Honor the בִּכּוּרִים of the wheat קָצִיר, read the book of Ruth and study the תּוֹרָה.	Ex. 19:1, 20:1- 17, Ex. 34:22, Lev. 23:15-22, Num. 28:26 שָׁבוּעוֹת is a celebration of GOD's provision-especially the בִּכּוּרִים of the wheat קָצִיר. A remembrance of the giving of the תּוֹרָה on Mt. Sinai.	שָׁבוּעוֹת Pentecost/Weeks 6th day of 3rd month (Sivan) 50 days after the Sabbath of Passover May

שָׁמוֹר	זָכוֹר	מוֹעֵד
The שׁוֹפָר is blasted, there is a מִקְרָא־קֹדֶשׁ and no work. Traditionally, the Jewish New שָׁנָה begins the ten יָמִים of repentance called "The יָמִים of Awe."	Lev. 23:23-25, Num. 10:10, Num. 29:1-6 יְהוָה doesn't give a reason for this celebration although He tells us to remember the רֹאשׁ חֹדֶשׁ (new moon of each Biblical month) with the sound of the shofar.	יוֹם תְּרוּעָה Day of Blasting (Rosh Hashanah) 1st day of 7th month (Tishrei) September/October
Both native and foreigners are to עָנָה their souls and do לֹא מְלָאכָה. Traditionally, Jews observe a צוֹם from food for 24 hours and attend a מִקְרָא־קֹדֶשׁ.	Lev. 16:29-31, 23:26-32 This מוֹעֵד, a יוֹם, קָדוֹשׁ is a fast day of judgement, כִּפֻּר, and forgiveness, when Israel's High priest went into the קָדוֹשׁ of Holies, took the blood of the sacrifice to make כִּפֻּר for the nation of יִשְׂרָאֵל.	יוֹם הַכִּפֻּרִים Day of Atonement (Yom Kippur) 10th day of 7th month (Tishrei) September/October
Dwell in temporary סֻכּוֹת for שִׁבְעָה יָמִים. The first and last יָמִים are a שַׁבָּת rest. Traditionally, to celebrate the קָצִיר, a שִׂמְחָה with לוּלָב and אֶתְרוֹג are waived daily.	Lev. 23:33-44, Zech. 14:16 סֻכּוֹת is considered the greatest מוֹעֵד, remembering the provision of יְהוָה as He led יִשְׂרָאֵל through the desert for 40 years. סֻכּוֹת also celebrates the end of the קָצִיר season.	סֻכּוֹת Feast of Tabernacles 15-21st day of 7th mo. (Tishrei) September/October